Lead with CARE

How Successful Leaders Manage Happy, Effective Teams with Concern, Authenticity, Realism, and Empathy

by Ely Albalos

HOW ② CONQUER

Published by How2Conquer
Atlanta, Georgia
www.how2conquer.com

How2Conquer is an imprint of White Deer Publishing, LLC
www.whitedeerpublishing.net

First edition, February 2024
Ebook edition created 2024
Illustrations and cover design by Telia Garner
Edited by Lauren Kelliher, Charlotte Bleau

Library of Congress Cataloging-in-Publication Data is on file at the Library of Congress, Washington, DC.

Print ISBN 978-1-945783-24-1
Ebook ISBN 978-1-945783-34-0

To my wife, who serves as my lighthouse, TQM. With you by my side, my wife, I want for nothing and what follows could never have been achieved without you.

To the Lord, Jesus Christ, for giving me a wonderful family that gives me purpose every day.

Contents

List of Figures and Tables

Preface

Entering the foyer, after speaking in front of 180 attendees at a church conference, my pastor approached me and said, "If I had known you could speak like that, I would have used you more often." I humbly smiled and responded, "That's why I never let you know beforehand."

I have spent the better part of my adult life comfortable with speaking to large crowds and stepping up to take control of a situation when it's deemed necessary. Most would acknowledge my abilities and determine I was born with a natural ability for leadership. While there may be some truth to that assessment, I have intentionally spent over 15 years improving the art of leadership.

Thrust into rooms with C-suite executives of Apple, Facebook, and Google domestically and internationally, I've been able to witness leadership at the most senior levels of the largest companies in the world. The exposure to ethically sound leaders and adopting their principles for leading sparked a passion within me that I had never known existed.

Once I developed my leadership "soft" skills, I sought to expand my "hard" skills by obtaining a master's degree and doctoral degree in areas of leadership. Throughout my academic journey I realized how much I still didn't know about leadership. Given my work experience and accrued education, I wondered, if I still felt like there was so much that remained to be learned, then how must others feel without as much?

After much deliberation, and inspiring nudges from my wife, I decided to reflect on my early career, identifying all the "I wish I knew . . ." moments as I moved up the leadership ranks. I started writing down my experiences and thoughts in no particular order. Before I knew it, what I had before me was the rough draft for *Lead with CARE*.

I never had designs on becoming an author, but after reviewing everything I had written down I couldn't deny it. I'll humbly admit I don't feel like there's anything particularly spectacular about what follows, but in the same breath I'll tell you what I'm sharing will make you a better leader. Everyone can adopt the skills and practices I share in this book. Everything in this book is practical and born out of my experience applying the same skills within corporate tech companies.

Leadership is a journey — one I enjoy taking part in while guiding others. My hope is that by the time you're done with this book, you'll have a few golden nuggets of information to elevate your own leadership abilities.

Introduction

If you picked up *Lead with CARE*, you're seeking answers for becoming a successful corporate leader. If you approach leadership with Concern, Authenticity, Realism, and Empathy, then you can break down barriers in friendships, relationships, the workplace, and society in general.

> **A leader can be successful in any environment when they have concern for those that work for and with them, are authentic in their approach, realistic with their own capabilities and the capabilities of others, and empathetic toward everyone.**

While there are many management books to choose from, my focus is people management in the corporate environment. Whether you're a new leader, an existing leader, or making the transition into the corporate environment, I have many takeaways that can and will transform your leadership skills.

Successful Leaders CARE

The primary philosophy of my book is that all successful corporate leaders should have **CARE** as their *raison d'être* (reason for being).

CONCERN
AUTHENTICITY
REALISM
EMPATHY

Everything in *Lead with CARE* revolves around having concern for employees, achieving authenticity in your approach, being realistic with capabilities and expectations, and expressing empathy when needed. I've broken down the book into four dedicated sections that take a deeper dive into the elements of CARE.

Have Concern: Introduction to People Management

This section is all about establishing a foundational understanding of people management and identifying your own leadership values. People management is the leader's ability to motivate, train, and guide their employees and teams. As a leader, you'll guide employees to reach their full potential. I'll teach you to express concern with awareness of culture and its impact on employees.

Be Authentic: Leadership Styles

Every successful corporate leader should understand the variety of leadership styles in their industry and try to identify a style that resonates with them. In this section, I introduce some of the most common styles along with their benefits and pitfalls. Different styles work for different managers, and they may need to be modified for specific direct reports, but the most important thing is to be authentic.

Be Realistic: Development and Goal Setting

You have an amazing opportunity to contribute to another person's professional success, but that only happens with feasible goal setting. With the trend brought on by the "great resignation," you must make every effort to maintain an employee's interest for the long term to lead with CARE. This means appealing to an employee's intrinsic motivation and continuing their development, so they envision the many ways forward within a company. This section discusses the ways performance development can assist with sustained employee performance and commitment for the long term.

Express Empathy: Communication

As a leader, it's essential that you communicate understanding of what others are feeling. The tricky part is that great communication is hard. This section examines the nuances of both verbal and nonverbal communication and explains the transactional process that occurs as two parties send and receive information across a medium. Given the many methods for communication, the key for a successful corporate leader will be to know how to meet employees where they are.

Know that my raison d'être for *Lead with CARE* is to show I CARE for leaders who are new to people management, feel lost in their leadership journey, or just want to be better at their job. I want them to know that even if they're feeling lost, they're not alone.

The philosophies in this book will improve your ability to become a successful corporate leader. If I had access to this information earlier in my career, I could've bypassed a lot of heartache and prevented countless mistakes. Congratulations on taking a huge step toward becoming a successful corporate leader who leads with CARE — picking up this book. I look forward to our journey together.

> **All obstacles can become opportunities for us to achieve our goals.**

Have Concern:
Introduction to People Management

I don't know if many people wake up one morning and announce to the world, "I'm going to be a leader someday." I know I didn't. My appetite for leadership developed over time. Though I was very active in student body programs in high school, I didn't start participating out of a natural inclination to lead — I was much more focused on appeasing my mother, who wanted to help bolster my college applications, so I could become the first member of my family to attend a university.

But my mother only nudged me once, at the very beginning, toward student body programs. Once I got settled in my roles, it was my own desire that kept me coming back for more each year. Maybe it was my innate ability to comfortably speak in front of a group of strangers, but I enjoyed leading people. Even more surprising, I enjoyed when people voluntarily followed my lead.

It took many years of training and education to realize there's a distinction between leading people who are forced to follow you and leading people who make the conscious decision to follow you. Unbeknownst to my high school self, I was enjoying my first reciprocal leader-follower relationship.

As Vince Lombardi once said, "Leaders are made, they are not born. They are made by hard effort, which is the price which all of us must pay to achieve any goal that is worthwhile" (Holden). If you were to look for quantitative data that tries to confirm this quote, you'd find mixed results on the matter. For our purposes, I agree with Vince Lombardi. Being a leader isn't an all-or-nothing, either-you-have-it-or-you-don't quality. With the right amount of motivation and desire, anyone can be a successful corporate leader. Not everyone will want to put in the hard effort or pay the price to be a successful corporate leader.

If done right, a leader acts like the sun to their employees, who are like seeds planted in a pot. A seed is immersed in soil for its nutrients, taking in water from its surroundings, but without the sun, the seed will never reach its full potential. The sun's energy allows the seed to grow and blossom. The sun by itself is a relentless force, but without a purpose it's just a ball of gas. By energizing a seed into a plant, the sun can give life to something that will flourish.

By leading with **CARE** you will be able to nourish those around you, energizing them so they can flourish to their full potential.

Each chapter's first reference to an acronym is stylized. Remind yourself of each term meaning in the "Acronym Glossary" on page 205.

It'll be hard to get people to voluntarily follow you if they don't feel like you have concern for them as individuals. I will teach you how to express concern by identifying the many types of working relationships that require it, discussing the impact of culture on employees, and outlining some key ethical considerations to keep in mind.

Chapter 1: What Does It Mean to Be a Leader?

I love leading people. I don't enjoy it because of the authority or perceived power. Instead, I see it as an opportunity to help others along their career path. I love to help guide others toward their aha moments of overcoming an obstacle, making a discovery, or just completing what may have seemed like an impossible task.

I love to see people demonstrate strength in areas they were previously weak and to see their confidence overflow into other areas of their life. Most of all I love working with a team that's operating on "all cylinders" with each member leveraging their strengths for the greater good. For a team to operate at its fullest potential, people management is key.

What Is People Management?

The term "people management" is used in this book as an action and responsibility, not a title or quality. Exactly as it sounds, people management is the broad category that mainly includes the soft skills associated with managing other people. Those soft skills include accountability, goal setting, leadership development, recruitment, and retention planning. There are countless soft skills associated with people management, and some of those skills are industry specific. People management is the leader's ability to motivate, train, and guide their employees and teams.

We set managers up for failure when we assume that if a person does a job well, they'll be able to supervise others doing that job just as well. That's where most people get it wrong. Just because a person is amazing at doing their job doesn't necessarily mean they will be just as successful at people management. Let me give you a personal example.

Back in my early days working as a security guard at Adobe Systems, I was an amazing employee (if I do say so myself). I dressed to impress, interacted with people in a professional manner, and made sure to fulfill all my daily obligations. I was also a team player who would stay late, come in early, or work an extra day to cover an opening.

In fact, I did my job so well that I was promoted to a supervisor on the night shift. That promotion was the first time I'd been given the responsibility of managing others. I was super excited, but there was one predicament. I had no training whatsoever. My only qualifications to be a supervisor were being good at my job and knowing the ins and outs of the company and organization.

When the day arrived, I reported to my first shift as a supervisor with a nice new tie and well-shined shoes, and I was expected to manage others. I had no idea what to do, and I had no context to understand what was different from my previous role. I wasn't given any training to know what the role of "supervisor" entailed, let alone any guidance on how to manage people. I didn't last long in that role. I had employees who weren't showing up for work, I didn't know how to hold people accountable, and I didn't understand how to motivate or develop those who did show up. It was one of my first failures as a leader and people manager.

You see this in every industry, and it may even be the case for some of you readers. (If this describes you, kudos to you for picking up *Lead with CARE*.)

An employee becomes a superstar as an individual or independent worker, and as a result they receive a promotion only to fail at people management. You can't blame the employee. The opportunity to manage others, even when the opportunity is a bit premature, is often too good to pass up.

Deciding to Lead

To be a successful corporate leader, you must make the conscious decision that you want to be in the business of people management. Like a business, you'll constantly be engaged in talent acquisition, retention, and development. More importantly you'll be dealing with lots of personalities. Some will be easier to deal with than others.

There are four important factors to consider when determining if you want to "people manage" as a leader, because there's no successful corporate leadership without people management.

People management is a **SURE** thing. It is:

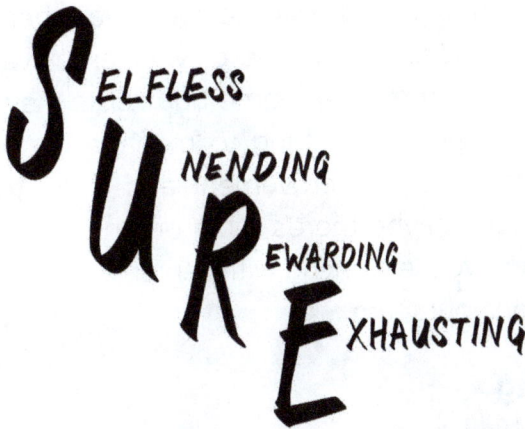

$$S \text{ELFLESS}$$
$$U \text{NENDING}$$
$$R \text{EWARDING}$$
$$E \text{XHAUSTING}$$

Selfless

When managing people, you must act selflessly. Other than an organization succeeding by directly benefiting from the output of an employee's actions, there's no immediate benefit from managing people. Knowing this, leaders must not get into this type of work for themselves. Instead, people management is meant to be a selfless act. Whether it's being an ally, advocating for employee development, or sponsoring a promotion, your priority is to put the needs of others before your own.

Unending

Being selfless may seem more altruistic than you'd like, but the good news is, opportunities to serve others as a leader are unending. When you gain responsibility for another person's career and livelihood, a successful corporate leader will selflessly and unendingly seek ways to serve their employees. Trust me, it's worth it in the long run, especially when you start to consider opportunities that work to improve diversity, equity, and inclusion.

There could be a new project on the horizon, and you might be actively attempting to position someone for the role because of their talent, knowing it could lead them on a path to their career goal. Maybe one of your employees is going through personal turmoil at home but insists they don't need time off work. Or you're trying to manage performance for someone who needs improvement and is on the verge of losing their job. Maybe there's a big organizational change in the works, and you're working with senior leadership to reduce the impact on your team.

Rewarding

Not only will your organization benefit from the un-ending investment in employees, but you'll start to realize the work is extremely rewarding. For many leaders, including me, contributing to another person's career success is its own reward.

As a leader you can invest in employee development, offer guidance via knowledge sharing, and position employees to successfully grow into bigger and better opportunities. Watching your employees become better versions of themselves is rewarding all on its own. Without a selfless, dedicated corporate leader, many employees are left floundering, always wanting something more but never being able to attain it.

Exhausting

Ultimately, people management in leadership is exhausting. As a leader, people management will take up a large portion of your time. Especially because, try as you might, you won't always get it right. If you're truly invested in your people, you'll constantly be looking for ways to provide them with, among other things, new opportunities, skill development, and new ways to leverage their strengths — and all this before your own priorities, work demands, and personal influences.

With great responsibility comes great responsibility, and it requires a whole bunch of your energy and effort. There will be times when you realize you're exhausted, but the only way to demonstrate **CARE** for employees is by staying right there with them — ready to motivate, train, and guide.

Don't worry, all is not lost. You're not alone in your quest to become a successful corporate leader. I'll introduce essential skills that will help you on your journey.

Just because you do a job well doesn't mean you're ready for people management. If you think you're ready, you need to be SURE. Once you're SURE, you're ready to start thinking and operating like a successful corporate leader.

Leading vs. Managing

It's important to understand the distinction between a leader and a manager. A leader is one who lends positive influence, inspiration, and motivation to a shared vision or purpose. A manager is focused purely on functions such as planning, operations, and controlling daily responsibilities of people, all with a focus on meeting short term objectives.

Think of a sports team. The leader is the talented athlete appointed as captain. They aren't directly managing other players, even though others may turn to them for inspiration and motivation. A manager would be the coach on the sideline with the clipboard, calling plays and making changes to team members in play.

Sometimes leaders can be managers, and managers can be leaders. You may have a captain (leader) on a sports team who makes audibles on the fly or directly calls to have players changed out, or you may have a coach (manager) who inspires players with motivating speeches.

A successful corporate leader is one who exercises the responsibilities of a manager. This distinction is essential to keeping the right leadership mindset. If you're a leader first, your primary focus will always be to guide and inspire others.

Creating Psychologically Safe Environments

Psychological safety is the ability to show up as your authentic self in the workplace and freely express your fears, discuss concerns, ask challenging questions, and share ideas without fear of repercussion or judgment. There are two qualities that will aid you in developing psychologically safe environments. They are acknowledging your limits and expressing vulnerability.

You may be wondering, as I used to, why acknowledging your limits is so important. You could even be worried that sharing them with your team might demonstrate weakness. That type of mentality will limit your true potential, and you could end up with polarizing relationships instead of prospering ones.

Leaders tend to pride themselves on dealing with adversity quietly. It's a badge of honor to avoid admitting that they have limits. They push themselves to the brink of failure before asking for help.

In reality, sharing your weaknesses expresses your vulnerability in the presence of others and serves as an example for them to do the same. This type of action creates an environment of psychological safety.

Personally, I have two well-known limits I share with my team regularly. The first is: I don't schedule meetings requiring concentrated cognitive investment after lunch. The second: I don't like meetings that are longer than one hour. As for the former, I know that I operate at my peak mental performance in the morning. After lunch, despite my best efforts, my full cognitive functions are no longer available. As for the latter, I'm not one who can sit still for very long. If a meeting needs to be longer than an hour, I ask that there be built-in, ten-minute breaks each hour.

Why do I feel it's important for my team to understand my limits? It's not because I want to exercise my authority and force them to respect my limits, it's because I don't have control over how my mind and body respond in the described situations, and employees benefit from knowing that. If they have an important presentation that requires my full attention, I want them to know they should schedule the meeting for the morning and to include breaks if it needs to be longer than an hour.

Rather than hide my limits and risk being disrespectful to my employees with inattention or exhaustion, I want them to know how to best position themselves within our working relationship for an optimal opportunity for success. By sharing, I'm demonstrating to others that it's okay to have limits and be open about them without fear of judgment.

The thought of being vulnerable in the workplace could cause some people to shudder and run for the hills. Don't worry, I'm not advocating you share your deepest and darkest secrets. Instead, I'm hoping to take the pressure off successful corporate leaders who think they're above asking for help. If you've built an appropriate team of talented individuals, then you don't have all the answers and should be asking for help. Otherwise, why hire other people? Demonstrating vulnerability with TAPE is invaluable aid for a successful corporate leader to have concern for themselves in the presence of others.

Vulnerability should hold your organization together like **TAPE** through:

TRUST

ASKING FOR HELP

PRIORITIZING YOUR NEEDS

ENTRUSTING YOUR TEAM TO DELIVER

Trust

Trust is the foundation of any relationship, but it's hard to earn and easy to lose. For leaders, trust can be earned by demonstrating vulnerability because it helps to acknowledge that you're not infallible. There's a common fallacy that leaders have everything worked out. Trust begets trust. If you expect your employees to trust you, then you must first trust them as knowledge holders of your vulnerabilities and limitations.

Asking for Help

Another way to contribute to the creation of trust is by asking for help. This simple action is perhaps the hardest for most leaders, especially new leaders. Since so many expect themselves to know everything, asking for help can seem to violate a kind of moral code. Asking for help goes hand in hand with knowing your limits. By asking your team for help, you're empowering their belief in their abilities. You're also creating an environment of trust because you're asking them to do something you aren't capable of while being open and transparent about it.

Prioritizing Your Own Needs

Prioritizing your own needs can go a long way toward contributing to vulnerability through trust because it shows you have concern for your well-being. One way to establish well-being is with your work-life balance.

Work-life balance is the equilibrium between how much work a person does and their personal needs such as hobbies, family time, or a much-needed vacation.

The amount of stress a leader accumulates from work can be debilitating. Serving as a role model, you must value prioritizing your own needs from time to time. Stepping away demonstrates to your team that you're willing to exercise concern for yourself and recharge.

Entrusting Your Team to Deliver

Stepping away to prioritize your own needs also shows that you entrust your team to deliver in your absence. When you're not around, you can hand off elements of your work to your employees, allowing them to represent you and develop their skills in the process while demonstrating that you don't always need to be the person running the show and are confident and secure enough in your position that you can let your team have some time in the limelight. Like acknowledging your limits, this type of trust can be hard for some leaders.

I know some leaders will be concerned with job security when stepping away, so to that I offer a couple perspectives:

- **If you're a successful corporate leader, then shouldn't you also be feeling invested in by your own leader and gaining new skills to take you to the next level? If that's the case, then what is there to be afraid of?**
- **At some point you'll have an opportunity to move on, and what better way to do it than by having someone on your team ready to fill your shoes?**
- **If you're feeling insecure about giving your employees opportunities, you need to revisit your desire to be a leader. Maybe you aren't so SURE that people management is for you.**

Key Takeaways

1	People management should be a **SURE** thing. It's selfless, unending, rewarding, and exhausting.
2	A leader is one who guides others through positive influence, inspiration, and motivation toward a shared vision or purpose.
3	The ability to acknowledge limits and express vulnerability aids you in developing psychologically safe environments.
4	Vulnerability should hold an organization together like **TAPE** through: trust, asking for help, prioritizing your needs, and entrusting your team to deliver.

Chapter 2: Types of Working Relationships

Now that we've established a working understanding of what it means to be a leader, and we're **SURE** it's the business we want to be in, certain types of working relationships might require you to adjust your support. Considering the various potential backgrounds employees will have, you need to understand there's no one-size-fits-all approach to every relationship as a successful corporate leader.

Some relationships have legal guidelines that must be respected, such as working with a contractor as opposed to a company employee. Certain relationships require different approaches, necessitating adjustments to a successful corporate leader's response.

Definitions of Working Relationships

Because the corporate environment, especially corporate tech, has nuances that could prove problematic for new leaders, it's important to understand the various classifications of working relationships. This section includes definitions of classifications you could encounter in the corporate environment. Some of the following definitions might have different names depending on where you work. Regardless of the name, the relationship is the same, and that's what's important to understand.

Independent Contractor (IC)

Often self-employed, an independent contractor (IC) typically works for a fixed term with a focus on a specific deliverable. It's important to understand that ICs might be told by the hiring company what they need to produce and the work expected of them, but the hiring company isn't allowed to dictate exactly how the result, or work, is achieved. There are very specific IRS implications as to how a company interacts with ICs.

Contractor/Vendor

Contractor and vendor are often synonymous, but both are much different than an IC. Contractors/vendors often work for a contracted company/employer and not for themselves. This means that they are actual employees of someone else but doing work for the hiring company.

The most common example of this in corporate companies is janitorial and kitchen staff. Contractors/vendors are prolific throughout corporate tech companies because they provide access to a talent pool that allows a hiring company to quickly reduce or increase without the costly task of making everyone a full-time company employee.

Part-Time Employee

A part-time employee is an employee who's directly hired into a hiring company but works less than the state mandated hours needed to be considered a full-time employee.

The number of hours can vary by state, so make sure you are well versed in your state's mandated requirements. Most states consider working less than thirty-two hours per week to be part-time.

Not all corporate tech companies have part-time employees, but for those that do, it's extremely important to pay attention to labor laws that dictate required breaks, lunches, and maximum number of work hours allowed.

Full-Time Employee

A full-time employee is an employee who's directly hired into a hiring company and works the minimum number of state-mandated hours needed to be considered a full-time employee.

The number of hours can vary by state, so make sure you are well versed in your state's mandated requirements. Most states consider working more than thirty-two hours per week to be full-time. Typically, full-time employees work forty hours per week.

Full-time employees make up the core staff within a corporate tech company, but there's a unique classification for full-time employees you must pay attention to. Some full-time employees are exempt from accruing overtime, and some are non-exempt. Hourly employees are non-exempt and allowed to accrue overtime pay. Salaried employees are exempt and not allowed to accrue overtime pay. This is important for leaders to know because hourly employees are subject to the same labor laws as part-time employees that dictate required breaks, lunches, and maximum number of work hours allowed, while salaried employees might not be.

Incentives

The focus of *Lead with CARE* is corporate tech, but many corporate environments offer enticing incentives for part-time and full-time employees, the obvious being generous compensation packages that consist of a corporate salary, bonus(es), and equity (in the form of company stock).

The other appeals are the almost endless fringe benefits such as free food, snacks, transportation, gyms that make private clubs look like public playgrounds, health/well-being and medical benefits, the list goes on and on. These benefits are where relationships get murky. Independent contractors (ICs) and contractors/vendors are not allowed to be granted all the benefits available to company employees.

In fact, not only are some benefits off limits, but the way you interact with ICs and contractors/vendors also has restrictions.

When an IC is hired, the hiring company can dictate the work expectations but not how the work gets done. For example, if a financial consultant is hired as an IC for their auditing expertise, the hiring company will sign a contract that outlines the desired deliverable within an allocated amount of time and a very specific scope of work.

If the hiring company doesn't intrude on the day-to-day work or dictate on a regular basis how the IC completes their work, there won't be a problem. However, if the hiring company starts to work intimately with the IC, and the IC believes they're working as a company employee when they're not hired as an employee, there can be some serious legal ramifications.

Another workplace compliance risk common in corporate tech companies is something known as co-employment. Co-employment refers to the obligations two companies share when one is the employer and the other is the contracted recipient (aka the hiring company) of a service provided by a contractor/vendor. Unlike an IC, a hiring company is allowed to dictate the day-to-day functions of a contractor/vendor, but there's a fine line.

Anything that has to do with human resources (HR) functions like hiring, firing, work assignments, payroll, or employee grievances must be handled by the contractor/vendor employer, not the hiring company. If a hiring company starts to treat said contractor/vendor like an employee and intrude on HR functions, a co-employment violation could occur, and (like with an IC) the hiring company could be subject to legal ramifications.

It's important to understand how these working relationships are classified within these working constructs. While you may be a successful corporate leader who wants to lead with **CARE**, there will be limitations and a need to adjust your approach. Let's examine how some of these working relationships could play out.

Employee-Employee Relationships

Aside from the nuisances of working with exempt and non-exempt employees, all types of workers can be treated the same since they're under the same company umbrella and subject to the same HR and performance expectations. This makes it easy to navigate the relationship and exercise CARE on a regular basis.

Whether a person is full-time or part-time, you can interact via 1:1 meetings, provide regular performance guidance, and exercise empathy if an employee approaches with a personal issue. The same cannot be said about a leader navigating an IC or contractor/vendor relationship.

Leadership in IC or Contractor/ Vendor Relationships

The way a company leader interacts with an IC or contractor/vendor can make a world of difference. Of the listed relationships, the easiest to understand is working with an IC.

An IC is a temporary staff member serving a specific purpose. When operating with CARE, you need to tread lightly with how much personal concern you show an IC. Not because you need to be heartless, but because you need to respect the legally binding contractual agreement.

You can still be authentic in your approach and use clear communication by dictating expectations, but you can't treat an IC like an employee. This type of relationship can seem disingenuous, but that's the legal nature of the agreement.

In a contractor/vendor relationship there's a little more wiggle room but not a lot. Most large corporate tech companies will have specific company divisions dedicated to ensuring contractor/vendor well-being. This makes sense in the grand scheme of things. Since a hiring company can choose to terminate the working relationship at any time, companies want to ensure they're maintaining corporate social responsibility (CSR) and not allowing a contractor/vendor group to be exploited for their services.

This helps a successful corporate leader because they can still operate with CARE but in a way that relieves some of the co-employment risk. For example, if a contractor/vendor approaches a leader of the hiring company with a personal issue, the leader can show concern and empathy by listening but then immediately ensure the issue is escalated to the correct company division to handle the issue. As long as the leader doesn't attempt to resolve contractor/vendor issues themselves, they'll be in the clear.

The most important takeaway is that regardless of the relationship, you must ensure to adjust their response to the situation. How you express CARE should depend on the staff member you're interacting with. Once you can successfully navigate the multiple types of relationships you'll encounter within corporate tech companies, you will have overcome one of the biggest hurdles managers face in this environment.

Key Takeaways

1	Independent contractors (ICs) and contractors/vendors aren't allowed to be granted all the benefits available to company employees.
2	You should tread lightly with how you show personal concern for non-employees because you need to respect labor laws and legally binding contractual agreements; you can't treat an IC or contractor/vendor like an employee.
3	Regardless of the relationship, you must adjust your response to a situation and how you express **CARE** depending on the staff member you're interacting with.

Chapter 3: What's Up with Culture?

There's a saying that goes, "culture eats strategy for breakfast." This phrase means that while a company could have the most elaborate short-, medium-, and long-term business plans, the internal company culture is the true determining factor of success.

Culture can affect the way an employee works, interacts, and leads. If the culture is one that has unreasonable expectations of employee contributions, enforces barriers around open communication, or lacks leaders who **CARE**, a company's ability to meet their corporate business plans is at risk. Therefore, it's important that you understand the importance of culture.

Having concern, being authentic, being realistic, and expressing empathy can serve as the cornerstones for building a positive company culture.

What Is Culture?

Culture is crucial to effectively leading an organization, so we can't talk about successful leadership without talking about culture.

For now, we'll define culture as, "a set of shared beliefs, behaviors, customs, traditions, and socially accepted standards." That definition is easy enough to understand, but the way it plays out in a corporate environment is complicated.

Depending on your industry you might discover some cultures are hierarchical with strict promotion guidelines, or perhaps they're competitive, creating an "every person for themselves" environment, or maybe they're so unstructured with an undeveloped management structure that you won't know which way is up. Not every cultural environment will work for every person, so self-awareness is key.

Ultimately, if you're looking to build a long-lasting and meaningful career with a company, you better have an idea of where you fit within the company culture, because you'll need to live and breathe that culture to thrive — and if you don't like it or can't acclimate, you won't last very long.

Culture Affects How You Work, Interact, and Lead

With all the amazing benefits of a corporate environment comes the demands of a challenging and ever-changing environment. Not only must you be among the top talent for any role you apply for to even be considered, but you also must maintain top performance throughout your time on the job. Once onboarded, most will be in for a wild ride. Depending on the role, if you can prove yourself victorious, then you'll sharpen your skills, create long-lasting relationships, and potentially be part of making history. Among all the opportunities for heroism, there's a snake in the grass: culture.

Think back to all those benefits I listed. Great salaries with amazing fringe benefits come with a cost; nothing is free. This is where some people can get confused. Culture is not made up of flashy perks. Those are just icing on the cake. Culture is created from company beliefs, behaviors, and socially accepted standards.

For example, for someone like me with a background in corporate security with global responsibility, sometimes there's no off switch. My schedule and the amount of work I need to do each day, week, or month are often dictated by the next global crisis. A person in my position is expected to be available at all times of the day, regardless of the day of the week or time of year.

The same can be said about an engineer who's working against tight timelines to roll out the next company product. My job, and maybe that of the engineer, can be subject to cyclical demands based on temporary crises, but some company cultures constantly keep their employees under sustained pressure with no off switch — ever.

High-performing companies will hire high performers like you. They will provide you with flashy perks to entice you and that can be a great thing. Heck, I've been in corporate tech for over a decade, and I love it, but the culture can be too much to handle depending on where you work.

As our society exited the COVID-19 pandemic and entered the endemic state, we experienced "the great resignation." Employees were tired of company cultures that demanded every moment of their time, regardless of the compensation and benefits, and required them to commute to work five days a week when other companies were taking a hybrid approach.

Some cultures can cause employees to experience burnout and force them to prioritize their job over their family because of unreasonable work expectations. Ultimately, everyone has a breaking point, and those who work in a poor company culture will find it sooner than others.

Positive Culture Starts on Day One

Building a positive company culture starts the first day a new employee joins a company. One mistake I see employees make, especially new employees, is not taking enough time to learn about the company culture. You can help facilitate this process right from the beginning. The "onboarding" experience of understanding the company and how it ticks is a crucial step a lot of employees miss because they're focused on trying to hit the ground running. This is a huge mistake and one that creates a culture of unrealistic expectations that convey the wrong message.

If culture does in fact eat strategy for breakfast, it makes sense that appropriate company culture should be cultivated within employees, particularly new employees, right from the start. However, it takes intentional effort to set realistic expectations right from the beginning and have enough concern for employee well-being to make sure employees don't feel the pressure to "hit a home run" on day one. In that way, you can help develop the company strategy that will pave the road to success and innovation and demonstrate your concern to employees.

Yet as most overachievers do, especially those in a corporate tech environment, the desire instead is to hit the ground running. It doesn't mean that things are a total loss. An employee can always slow down, step back, and learn what it's like to smell the roses, but it won't ever be the same. Let's use the example of a new car to illustrate this point.

Aside from the tedious paperwork, I love the excitement of shopping for a new car. I will do hours of research on the internet, talk to friends, talk to salespeople, and test drive a variety of cars until I find exactly what I want. I always remember the excitement of walking out of the dealership with car keys in hand, stepping into my new car, and driving it home for the first time. Of the entire experience the part I love the most is the new car smell — there's nothing like it.

You ever notice no matter what you do, at some point that new car smell will be gone? It could take months, years, or even days (depending on what you're doing in that car) but at some point, that smell will be gone, and no amount of detailing or air fresheners will capture the same scent as the day you drove it off the lot.

The same can be said about missing the opportunity of enjoying the "onboarding" experience as a new employee. You can never go back to experiencing the "newness" for the first time, so you must enjoy it while it lasts, because it will never be the same.

Possessing a vast understanding of culture and its impact on employee and company performance will help you by creating impactful organizations that operate with CARE.

Speaking from my experience at Meta, Apple, and Google, I can tell you that each one of those environments has a much different culture from the others. Transitioning from one culture to another required a purposeful investment in time to understand the company and to build the right relationships. If employees don't take an appropriate amount of time to adapt to company culture right from the start, a key opportunity may be lost.

Let me use my experience transitioning from Apple to Meta as an example.

Unlike Apple where privacy and secrecy were key with offices and cubicles abound, Meta's office spaces were completely open with minimal private offices and very few secluded cubicles. Instead, there were rows and rows of desks in a variety of configurations with nary a privacy divider separating one from another. The space for Meta's CEO was no different. This told me a lot about the company culture right from the get go.

Like the Meta platform, I was operating in a space of trust, transparency, and openness. During my first week, as part of my onboarding, I took part in my first company social event. The event served beer and appetizers, great fringe benefits if I do say so myself, leading up to a Q&A (Question and Answer) period with Meta CEO Mark Zuckerberg.

I was blown away by the fact that anyone who was a Meta employee could attend the Q&A, walk up to the mic, and ask the CEO any question on their mind. That first week at Meta was an entirely new experience for me, and I knew right then and there I couldn't operate by the same rules I had at Apple.

This was a great realization for me because I was willing to embrace the openness and felt that it suited my leadership style and preference for openly interacting with others. For me, I knew Meta was a great cultural fit, but I'm sure for some of you reading this book the idea of an almost carefree open environment might seem undesirable. That's what makes understanding culture so important.

As an employee, you'll be spending most of your waking hours in the workplace, so you better like the culture. As a successful corporate leader, you'll be leading and helping others navigate the company culture, so you better like it as well, so you can have concern for your employees and exercise CARE.

As a leader, you must take the appropriate amount of time to understand the corporate culture you're operating in, and more importantly, you must create an atmosphere in which you support new employees in their onboarding experience. Having done a few transitions in corporate companies and having hired hundreds of new employees and supported their onboarding, I often give people ninety days just to learn about the culture, company, and their role. I've heard new team members time and time again express their gratitude for providing a generous "ramp up," or acclimation, period.

Showing you have concern for employees by allowing them to embrace the company culture will be your first invaluable step toward becoming a successful corporate leader and contributing to the creation of a positive company culture.

Key Takeaways

1	Culture eats strategy for breakfast. A company could have the most elaborate short-, medium-, and long-term business plans, but the internal company culture is the true determining factor of success.
2	Flashy perks are not culture. Culture is created from shared beliefs, behaviors, traditions, and social standards.
3	Culture can affect things that might seem employee-specific, "personal" issues such as burnout, confidence, and general well-being.
4	You should facilitate a deep understanding of company culture during onboarding. Set realistic expectations and have concern for employee well-being to make sure employees don't feel the pressure to "hit a home run" on day one.

Chapter 4: Ethics and Why They Matter

The final element, and perhaps the most crucial, required for successful corporate leaders to show concern for others is ethics. Ethics help dictate how a leader and a company conduct business. Maintaining high ethical standards speaks volumes to employees.

The Bible states, "Do unto others as you would have done to you," (Luke 6:31) otherwise referred to as the "Golden Rule." The concept seems simple enough to understand, but it's often hard to abide by. The fact is, we're all emotional beings and successful corporate leadership is full of emotional triggers. Whether it's arrogance, ignorance, greed, jealousy, or embarrassment, the list of obstacles that stand in the way of being ethical is seemingly infinite.

A successful corporate leader will always be in a position to consider ethical behavior and equitable decision-making. That's the point of being **SURE** you want to lead others. There will be endless opportunities for your decisions to affect others downstream.

Perspectives of Ethical Behavior

Let's break down the perspectives of ethical behavior as a company, in a department, and as a leader. We'll look at examples for each to help understand why ethics are paramount in a corporate environment.

Company Ethics

The first perspective of ethical behavior seems like a no-brainer, yet time and time again we read and hear about companies' violations of ethical behavior. As an element of corporate social responsibility (CSR), company ethical responsibility is concerned with, among other things, how it treats its customers, investors, and employees.

While most companies do a fair job of remaining ethical, there are horror stories to be aware of. At the time of this writing, one company is making headlines regarding their unfair treatment of female employees who were subject to sexual harassment and abuse in what was called a "frat environment."

You must understand that if a company is more concerned with making a profit than they are with how their female employees are treated, there's no avoiding the creation of a toxic work environment that's impossible for leaders to overcome.

After all, if you're considering a leadership role, you hopefully understand that while your own personal morals might not align with the company, you'll serve as a representative of the company in the eyes of the people you're leading. You'll start to really understand how a company culture can affect employees, including you.

Department Ethics

Let's say that a company is operating in an ethical manner, maintaining its CSR with a positive image in society and no known inappropriate behavior. Within the brick and mortar or virtual office spaces of the company, another layer of complexity exists at the department level.

Where company ethics occur across the entire company, department ethics occur within a smaller subset of the company. For example, you could have an HR department that manages all HR issues for the company. Depending on the size of the company, that HR department could have many leaders managing other employees. The way all the leaders of the HR department collectively treat employees represents department ethics.

While unethical department behavior might not always bleed into the rest of the company, it can be just as toxic. You can think of department ethics as the ability to maintain equitable access to resources, information, job assignments, and promotional opportunity. Unethical behaviors within departments can take the shape of favoritism for premium job assignments, fast tracking promotions for men over women, or intentionally withholding access to leadership or resources, unfairly setting some up for failure.

Due to the close working relationships employees have within their department, department ethics often has the greatest impact on culture. There's a slogan in management that goes, "What you ignore, you condone." If you allow unethical behavior to take place within your immediate departmental purview, then the cascading message you're sending to your employees is that you don't care for their welfare. This is probably one of the worst messages a leader can send their department.

Another aspect of company culture you must consider is making SURE you're ready to step into a role as a leader in a department with questionable ethics. In navigating department ethics, your challenge is you're only one small fish in a larger pond. When working in a collective, there's only so much influence one leader has over others unless they're the most senior in the department. At times you might feel like you're fighting uphill battles when attempting to change poor department ethics, but sometimes you have no other choice when leading with **CARE**.

Leadership Ethics

Leadership ethics are simply the ethical codes an individual leader operates under. While they're not to be confused with the leadership style known as ethical leadership, there are some similarities. This is where the "Golden Rule" really starts to shine. While each individual leader's ethics may vary slightly, each should strive to operate with integrity, trust, honesty, and fairness.

Leadership ethics can be found inside and outside the workplace. They can be found in volunteer work, social circles, or even at home. Any time you're put in a position of trust and are responsible for leading others, how you respond in those positions is a measure of your leadership ethics. The good news is when you learn how to navigate the complexity of a corporate environment, by implementing the lessons in *Lead with CARE*, you can easily apply them to your social circles, volunteer work, and family.

As a successful corporate leader, you have direct influence over and control of your team. Whether it's allocating wage increases, determining firing/hiring decisions, or providing job resources for employees, you, as the leader, can make or break a person's career. Even more importantly, you can impact a person's livelihood. The information that follows in the remainder of this chapter will help you watch out for poor ethical behavior and encourage you to model great ethical behavior, optimizing the concern you have for your employees.

Fundamentals of Ethical Behavior

Now that we've laid the foundation to understand why ethics are critical for being a successful corporate leader, let's introduce some principles for ensuring ethical behavior. As a leader, you must constantly be aware of the ethical behavior of the company, department, and yourself because it all contributes to the corporate culture. In **Chapter 3: What's Up with Culture?**, I introduced the saying, "culture eats strategy for breakfast." As such, unethical behavior at any of the previously discussed levels will create barriers and inequity, but acting as an ethical leader will help break down barriers to pave the way for equity and inclusion.

You can act ethically with five simple principles and be the **DREAM** of ethical leadership with:

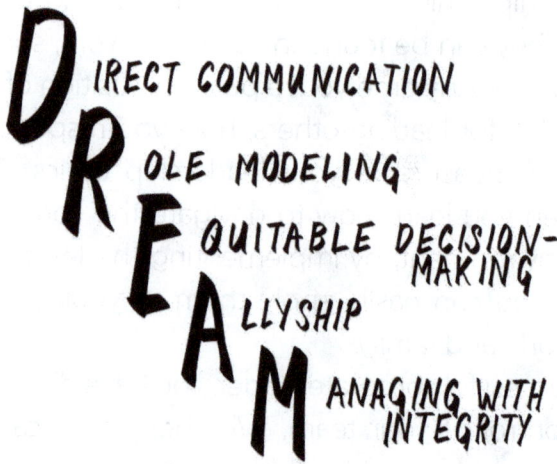

DIRECT COMMUNICATION

ROLE MODELING

EQUITABLE DECISION-MAKING

ALLYSHIP

MANAGING WITH INTEGRITY

Direct Communication

Direct communication, specifically transparent communication, is the most misunderstood tool a successful corporate leader has in their toolbox. Transparent communication means communication in all facets (be it face-to-face, phone, email, etc.) that's clear, precise, and free of ambiguity.

By transparent I'm not alluding to "all" information. I know you can't always reveal confidential information. Instead, I'm referring to the information that's necessary for your employees, or direct reports, to be able to do their job. This type of information should contain clear expectations through SMART goals (more on this in **Chapter 13: Performance Enablement**) and provide additional clarity when needed. It shouldn't be conveyed in a fashion that's designed to keep your people guessing or in the dark. It should also not be so prescriptive that you, as the leader, are bordering on being a micromanager.

You must hone the skill of transparent direct communication because it ensures everyone receives the same message from leadership, serving as a significant contributor toward diversity, equity, and inclusion initiatives. Being an ethical leader using direct communication means:

- **Not intentionally hiding necessary facts and details from your people**
- **Keeping employees in the loop when situations change**
- **Following up when information is dense**
- **Providing insight and context to help them reach understanding**

Role Modeling

Role modeling, or walking the walk, is a straightforward concept. A leader should model the behavior and characteristics they expect to see in others. Rather than reiterate the obvious regarding being a positive role model, I'll offer an important concept. When striving to create an environment rich with diversity, equity, and inclusion, an organization must ensure there are a variety of role models in leadership positions.

As an element of acting ethically, on a company and department level actions must be taken to ensure the population of those holding leadership positions is representative of the employee population and community being served. It does no good to have positive role models if they only represent the racial majority.

When seeking to create equity, role models in leadership must resemble a diverse population serving as a beacon for others to follow and emulate. Being an ethical leader acting as a role model means:

- **Demonstrating the change you want to see**
- **Providing equal opportunity for everyone**
- **Being authentic**
- **Representing the employee population**

Equitable Decision-Making

Equitable decision-making is making decisions using all facts available in a fair manner that considers individual situational context or actions. Understanding a few key terms will help you implement equitable decision-making practices regularly.

First, understand there's a difference between equality and equity. You can easily research these terms with a quick Google search, so I won't go into detail but instead will provide a practical understanding. Equality can be understood as making things equal across the board regardless of individual circumstances. Equity can be understood as creating fairness for people when considering their individual circumstances and needs. As a visual person, I'll support these definitions with a couple of images.

A   B

Based on the visual representation in image A, it's easy to see that equality means each plant has equal access to resources, or a spot by the window in this case. Based on a plant's individual circumstances, things may not really be equal. The shorter plant doesn't have equal access to the sun even though it was provided with the same spot as the other plants.

We see something different when we consider equity meaning each plant gets what they need to reach the sun. image B helps illustrate the fairness of equity, demonstrating how the redistribution of resources, providing plant stands, helps bring every plant up to an equitable level. Based on the individual's needs, a taller or shorter plant, given their situation — trying to reach the sunny window — each plant is given different resources — height of plant stand — to level the playing field.

Bringing this all together, an ethical leader cannot always respond the same way, in every situation, with the same solution. For example, if you were trying to improve diversity in your organization and posted a job advertisement, equality means posting the job advertisement online and waiting for anyone and everyone to apply. Equity, in this situation, means having recruiters actively target marginalized populations through job fairs, networking, and active outreach.

If we were to apply this concept to a promotional situation in the workplace, equality would mean that a promotional opportunity is listed on an internal job board for all to see and waiting for applicants until the deadline. Equity would mean sending that promotional opportunity directly to each potential eligible applicant, holding multiple information sessions, or offering shadowing opportunities to help applicants understand the role.

Equitable decision-making as an ethical leader includes:
- **Exhibiting fairness to everyone**
- **Thinking outside the box**

- **Challenging the status quo**
- **Recognizing the context of a situation**

Allyship

Being an ally means understanding your own strengths, advantages, and opportunities and recognizing when to leverage those benefits to help another. Allyship isn't done easily but with thoughtful execution, it can be a very powerful contributor toward ensuring ethical leadership.

Allyship is most relevant when helping those who have been traditionally marginalized. As a leader, if you're in an advantageous position because of your race, gender, or position of power, then you have an opportunity to be an advocate and ally for those including but not limited to women in male-dominated industries, members of the LGBTQ+ community, and Black, Indigenous, and People of Color (BIPOC).

Companies and organizations have started to take intentional action toward improving diversity, equity, and inclusion (DEI). As part of this new era of DEI, you need to know how to support the creation of inclusive environments and allyship. Implementing DREAM by including direct communication, role modeling, equitable decision-making, allyship, and managing with integrity will help you create an environment supporting DEI. It all culminates into being an ally whenever possible.

Finding opportunities to be an ally can be challenging and, if not accustomed to how it's done, can feel uncomfortable in the beginning. However, if you make your employees' interests a priority, then acting as an advocate (or ally) on behalf of others starts to become second nature. Being an ethical leader operating as an ally means:

- **Using your position of advantage to help others**
- **Having an interest in ensuring equity for all**
- **Not being afraid to step in for others**

- **Being genuine in your desire to help others who have been marginalized**

Managing with Integrity

Managing with integrity is a concept that most people understand. By managing with integrity, I mean leading others with honesty while maintaining strong moral principles. When managing with integrity there will be times when you'll have the ability to exercise absolute authority and influence over another's work and/or career.

You see this in two primary areas of the workplace: when hiring or firing employees and when determining wage increases or promotion. It's imperative you manage the career decisions of others with infallible integrity. For some it's easy to get distracted with the power to influence others, and for others it's too heavy of a burden to handle.

Regardless of where you fall once you're in a leadership role you must consistently manage with integrity to operate as a successful corporate leader. Being an ethical leader managing with integrity means:

- **Not taking situations personally**
- **Acting with fairness regardless of the individual**
- **Being neither power hungry nor afraid to act on others' behalf**
- **Considering all perspectives and acting only after all facts are understood**

While I hope it's not the case for everyone, this chapter may have been the hardest to come to terms with. I operate with the understanding that everyone attempts to bring their best ethical selves to the workplace, but sometimes the wrong decision, in a moment of weakness, leads people astray. Maintaining high ethical standards while leading with CARE will help reinforce positive and supportive workspaces for everyone.

Key Takeaways

1	Treat others the way you would expect to be treated.
2	Appropriate ethical behavior should occur at all levels including as a company, in a department, and as a leader.
3	Acting ethically is a core function for leaders in and out of the workplace.
4	Whether you're a leader in your social circles, volunteer work, or your family, using **DREAM** as principles of acting ethically will help improve your ability to become a successful corporate leader.

Chapter 5: Diversity, Equity, and Inclusion (DEI)

Diversity, equity, and inclusion (DEI) programs continue to receive a lot of attention and rightfully so.

The fact is that there are inequities in the workplace. Regardless of the structured framework applied to analyze the workplace and highlight the inequities, everyone can benefit from understanding the need for DEI. A successful corporate leader must be aware that members of their organization may have been marginalized at one point in their past. Even more challenging, a leader may be in the middle of a polarized environment struggling to make their own way, let alone helping their employees navigate their careers.

DEI initiatives are here to stay, and the only way to be successful is to approach DEI with a growth mindset. This chapter includes some best practices that will help newcomers understand DEI and potentially reduce apprehension about discussing it.

Cultural Consciousness

Cultural consciousness can be defined as the ability to effectively work with individuals from diverse cultures. It means developing meaningful relationships with others regardless of their background through an ongoing process that relies on self-reflection, self-awareness, and acceptance of cultural differences.

When employees bring their identity to work there may conflict with the organization's cultural "norm." Depending on the global footprint of the corporation you're operating in, you could be working with people from many different walks of life. Depending on who you're working with, you'll have to adapt your leadership approach to create a meaningful relationship with your employees.

Even if your company has a headquarters in the United States and employees across the globe, there's no one-size-fits-all approach to leadership. This concept is something not every leader is taught. Globalization of companies has led to the need for you to remain nimble and adapt your approach based on who you're working with.

In my leadership journey, I found two resources extremely valuable in the way they broadened my own cultural consciousness. I strongly encourage everyone serious about becoming successful corporate leaders to browse *Culture's Consequences: Comparing Values, Behaviors, Institutions and Organizations Across Nations* by Geert Hofstede as well as the GLOBE (Global Leadership and Organizational Behavior Effectiveness) research program.

Both studies introduce several cultural dimensions and offer comparisons of how and where some countries sit within the developed measurement scales. See the cultural dimensions that each offers for reflection in the chart below.

Cultural Dimensions Explained

Geert Hofstede's *Culture's Consequences*	The GLOBE Research Program
• Power Distance • Collectivism vs. Individualism • Uncertainty Avoidance Index • Femininity vs. Masculinity • Short-term vs. Long-term Orientation • Restraint vs. Indulgence	• Performance Orientation • Assertiveness • Future Orientation • Humane Orientation • Institutional Collectivism • In-group Collectivism • Gender Egalitarianism • Power Distance • Uncertainty Avoidance

It would take far too long to define all the dimensions in these resources, but as you can see in the chart there are some similarities. Let me provide an example from my own experiences that may help you understand the power of cultural consciousness.

I was born and raised in the United States, and when I worked for Apple, I started a project to oversee a site in Shanghai, China. At the time, I had never traveled to the Asia-Pacific region, and I was eager to take on the assignment. After my first couple trips to meet the team based in Shanghai, I quickly realized I had a lot to learn about working with people born and raised in China who had never been managed by an American.

Things came to a head six months into the project when I realized certain security design features I'd asked for weren't being built. I'd been dealing with a local project manager, and I thought our relationship was going well.

We had been in multiple meetings, and I had told him what I wanted done, and he would agree with a nod saying "yes, sounds good." However, he wasn't making the changes I asked for even though he agreed. I had to consult a peer who was adept at working with teams in China to understand what was going on. Low and behold, there was an issue of power distance and collectivism.

According to the GLOBE research program, power distance is the extent that people accept and endorse authority. According to Hofstede's *Culture's Consequences*, collectivism is the extent that people are loyal to the group they belong to.

In my meetings with the project manager, I was the leader representing maximum authority, power distance. When the project manager was saying "yes," he was deferring to my authority even though he couldn't provide what I was asking for. Yet to save face and maintain group harmony, or collectivism, the project manager couldn't say "no." I had to completely change how I approached project requests and align my interactions to match the culture I was operating in.

Once I understood how power distance and collectivism contributed to the project outcome, I was able to reduce their effects to create an open dialogue between me and the project manager. I was able to learn why my requests couldn't happen and found equitable solutions in their stead.

In my example, I was working abroad in a foreign country, but given the diverse workforce leaders operate in, nothing prevents the reverse from occurring. You could have someone from another country new to the United States attempting to assimilate. Depending on where they're from, cultural consciousness would be just as important.

Expanding your own cultural consciousness is the first step toward understanding how DEI initiatives take root. Self-reflection, self-awareness, and acceptance of cultural differences are paramount to creating organizations capable of successful change efforts.

Common Misconceptions about DEI

I want to dispel a couple of common misconceptions about DEI and creating environments that are diverse. The first is that some organizations assume that if they have a diverse workforce there will be a magical injection of diverse thinking. After all, you need only do a quick Google search to find a myriad of articles that talk about the value that diversity brings to the table for achieving innovation.

While I would love that to be true, it simply isn't the case. To lead with **CARE**, you must understand that having diversity in the workplace does not ensure diverse thought. There is no magical switch that gets flipped because you have a person of color, woman, or someone from another country sitting across from you. Trust me, if that were the case, then there would be no one ever marginalized; would there? The main reason for this is the second misconception.

The second misconception is that once you have one, two, or any number of people of color, or other marginalized community, in the organization you can say you are a diverse workforce. If you were looking at purely quantitative data within your organization, you might think that once you hit a certain percentage of people of color, let's say an amazing 50 percent (don't get distracted by the number; it's purely anecdotal), you're done, and diversity will be a mainstay through every facet of your global organization. However, what if that 50 percent of your workforce who are people of color only make up lower ranks within your organization and not senior leadership roles that remain dominated by a different race? You really couldn't say that qualitatively you were a diverse workforce.

I was in a doctoral class recently in which we were discussing equity. One of the students explained half-hearted attempts at obtaining equity within organizations for people of color as, "Being invited to the dance isn't the same as being asked to dance." The point they were making is that just because an organization hits a target number for people of color within their organization doesn't mean that they'll be accepted, valued, or integrated into a culture that's based on a different majority.

The minute you, as a successful corporate leader, embark on driving DEI initiatives within your organization, you're in it for the long haul, and while most corporate entities are focused on data and analytics, you can't judge improvements in diversity, equity, and inclusion solely on increasing numbers. The quality and fair treatment, assimilation, and acknowledgement of everyone, especially those who are historically marginalized, is more important than just increasing percentages.

Enough of the heavy stuff, let's learn more about how to support DEI within your organization as a successful corporate leader.

Supporting DEI in Your Organization

We'll start with some definitions, so we're on the same page. If DEI is of particular interest for you, I highly encourage researching its many facets and digesting several of the many educational programs offered from a variety of institutions.

Diversity	Differences among people based on their age, ethnicity, gender, race, socioeconomic status, etc.
Equity	Creating fairness for people when considering their individual circumstances and needs
Inclusion	Providing equal access to resources and opportunities to those who otherwise would've been excluded

Depending on your source, you'll see certain nuances to these definitions, but for our purposes, the definitions are sufficient. Now let's apply the definitions to the graphic on the next page, so we can gain a visual representation of how these concepts play out.

Starting with equity — since we already discussed this in **Chapter 4: Ethics and Why They Matter**, it will be the easiest to understand. The following graphic helps to illustrate the fairness of equity demonstrating how the redistribution of plant stands, or resources, help bring each plant up to an equitable level based on their needs.

C

Based on image C, we can assume that the plants pictured have the same need of sunlight. We can see that the plant on the left can easily reach the window without any aid. The plant in the middle requires more resources, in this case a short stand, to reach the window and gain equal standing as the plants to the left and right of it. The plant on the far right needs an even taller boost.

The smallest plant, hanging from above, requires a different type of resource. To gain an equitable standing as the three plants on the ground, a hanging pot is used as a resource to reach the window. The hanging planter is an example of inclusion, because had plant stands been provided, which would demonstrate equality, those specific resources would have still left the tiny plant excluded because its pot doesn't have a flat bottom. Every plant in the graphic is provided with the specific resources it needs to overcome the barrier, in this case the height of the window, to soak in the sunlight equitably.

Diversity represents the difference all four have from one another. Using our illustration, effective DEI can be viewed as the integration of the four plants in front of the window, with access to the sun, creating and environment of diversity, equity, and inclusion.

If you were to imagine your organization and the members within it and take the creative leap using the illustration above, you can start to see why DEI initiatives are so important. We can view this barrier to mean any number of things from socioeconomic challenges, gender inequality, or marginalization.

The sunlight on the other side of the barrier could be a job, promotion, or life goal that employees want to reach. The stool and plant stands represent the tailored resources your employees need to reach those goals. Even the person that has no stand may be suffering from cognitive load or a fixed mindset (more on these two concepts later) and while it doesn't look like they need a stand, they may require a different type of resource.

Ultimately your goal as a successful corporate leader is to understand how DEI initiatives can work to support an employee's potential and create a culture of belonging. The actions you take, whether they're implicit or explicit, sends a message to your employees about what matters to you. If you create an environment based on diversity, equity, and inclusion, your employees will have an easier time maintaining their motivation and will connect with their purpose within your organization.

At this point your mental load may be reaching its maximum because while this may sound all fine and good, it's a heavy lift, and you may feel you wouldn't even know where to start. To that I will revisit something I introduced at the start.

All successful corporate leaders have **CARE** as their raison d'être. Having concern for employees, achieving authenticity in your approach, being realistic with capabilities and expectations, and expressing empathy when needed is the foundation toward achieving DEI. The next skills I introduce will get you well on the way to creating an environment of diversity, equity, and inclusion.

Like a boat navigating through wind, you will forge ahead with DEI, knowing **TACK**:

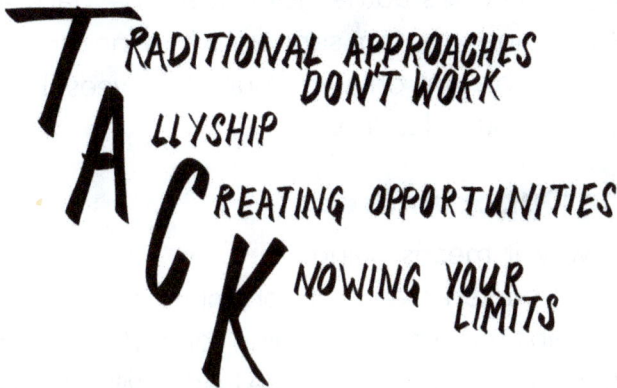

TRADITIONAL APPROACHES DON'T WORK

ALLYSHIP

CREATING OPPORTUNITIES

KNOWING YOUR LIMITS

Traditional Approaches Don't Work

There are a variety of research-based studies that suggest traditional approaches to DEI don't work. By traditional, I mean the mandatory diversity training all employees sit through on a regular basis, often annually. In fact, studies have shown that dissension is created from forced training by polarizing those who are in the racial majority because the training makes them feel like they're part of the problem when they otherwise wouldn't be. What was meant as a tool to foster inclusiveness is inadvertently stirring the pot. You can't rely on an annual video, training, or workshop to magically change the environment. If that was the case, DEI would have been solved years ago.

Allyship

Instead, take control of your own DEI efforts by starting with allyship. Allyship is a practice where one person in a position of influence can take meaningful action to support another. This has nothing to do with a position of "power." If you're witness to anyone being marginalized in a meeting, on a call, or even in an email, you can take action to change the tides. This doesn't mean that you're rescuing a person. Instead, it means advocating for a person when no one else will, supporting someone's authenticity when they face adversity, and listening and offering support when needed. You can accomplish all this not only for your employees, but also for peers and even other leaders.

Creating Opportunities

In a way, it means being **SURE** on a whole other level. Especially if you can create opportunities for others. The 'U' in SURE means there are "unending" opportunities for you to serve others. A successful corporate leader will always leverage their resources in a way that creates opportunities where others can thrive.

I had an opportunity to do this very thing for someone I was mentoring at Google, and the outcome was amazing. Google started a program to support the growth and development of women in my department. My department decided to focus on helping women because historically it was primarily dominated by men.

I had a wonderful opportunity to serve as a mentor to a participant for six months. My mentee had been with the company for twelve years but had not had an opportunity to progress very far in her career.

For six months, I helped her focus on strategic thinking, personal branding, and advocacy. When the mentorship was coming to an end, I was able to create a temporary assignment on my team. The mentee was a perfect selection for it, and I was able to select her for the assignment working on my team for six months.

The work she accomplished in six months should've taken someone a full year to complete. Not only was I able to have her complete high priority projects in a short time, but I also was able to position her so she was communicating and sharing updates with senior leaders in the department.

In a very short time, she was receiving amazing praise from all levels of the department, and her skills continued to improve along with her confidence. Based on the positive outcome of her experience, the work it took for me to create the opportunity, which was about eight weeks of administrative hoops, was worth it.

Know Your Limits

Regardless of how great you might be at being an ally and creating opportunities, you still need to know your limits when it comes to DEI initiatives. While cultural consciousness is rewarding, it can be daunting. When you layer on the idea of practicing allyship and creating opportunities for others, your head could really start to spin. That's why you need to know your limits. This book isn't meant to make you an expert on DEI. Honestly, I'm not an expert myself, but I know my limits.

Authenticity

I have three simple rules to **ADD** authenticity when it comes to exercising DEI in the workplace:

ACCEPT EVERYONE
DON'T FAKE IT
DO BE PRESENT

Accept Everyone

People come from all walks of life, and just like you would like to be accepted for who you are, be accepting of everyone else. A corporate leader will be exposed to different accents, clothing choices, ethnicities, nationalities, races, the list goes on and on. The only thing that's relevant for you as a successful corporate leader is how people do their job. When you can create a positive work atmosphere in a supportive company where your employees feel accepted for who they are, people will flourish and be able to positively impact everyone around them.

Don't Fake It

Fostering DEI and creating a supportive company and department atmosphere will be hard, but don't fake your knowledge. The fastest way to sabotage your success at creating an inclusive environment is to be inauthentic and act like you know everything about topics like race, gender, ethnicity, and culture. Those topics aren't mastered overnight.

Do Be Present

Regardless of your level of competence, when you focus on accepting everyone for who they are, do be present when others need you. Remember that creating an environment that supports diversity, equity, and inclusion doesn't mean you must agree with everyone about everything all the time. Instead, it means creating psychologically safe environments where people feel they can trust you as their leader to allow them to be their authentic and genuine selves.

Competence

There are four recognized stages of competence, broken down in the following chart, leaders need to be aware of.

Unconscious Incompetence (Ignorance)	Being unaware of your lack of skill or proficiency
Conscious Incompetence (Awareness)	Being aware of your lack of skill
Conscious Competence (Learning)	Being able to apply a skill with purposeful effort
Unconscious Competence (Mastery)	Being able to perform the skill automatically

Of the competences listed, the most worrisome is unconscious incompetence, in which a person is either unaware of their lack of knowledge or chooses to remain ignorant. Fortunately, by reading *Lead with CARE*, that one doesn't apply to you. Congratulations — you can consider yourself part of the consciously incompetent group because you're aware of your lack of skill and doing something about it. As you begin to learn more about leadership and DEI, you begin to edge to conscious competence by purposefully implementing the learned principles in this book.

Your learning efforts don't need to, and shouldn't, end after reading *Lead with CARE*. In matters of DEI, choose to be consciously incompetent and learn from additional sources until you're comfortably, consciously competent.

When you've mastered the DEI principles of *Lead with CARE* and skills from other sources, you'll be able to automatically, and unconsciously, perform without concentrated effort.

Recognize When Someone Has Accepted Marginalization

This is the perfect time to introduce a phenomenon I believe occurs not only in the workplace but also in day-to-day life. I have observed what I deem "accepted marginalization" in my life and the lives of others.

So far, everything including introducing the need for cultural consciousness, cultural dimensions, and knowing the fundamentals of equity have not been original ideas. I've taken a lot of my own education and leadership experience and concentrated it to its essentials in the hopes that you'll be inspired to have CARE, so that you can TACK-le DEI initiatives and ADD authenticity to the workplace.

I like to explain marginalization as a social construct where a person, group, idea, or associated actions and contributions are rendered powerless and insignificant. You might see marginalization in the workplace where well-qualified women are passed over for promotions in favor of men. There have been publicized incidents of marginalization in the film industry where female actors receive lower salaries than male actors. You will also witness marginalization in some social circles where one friend's ideas or needs seem to take priority over others.

Marginalization can occur within ingroup members, like those of the same race and gender, and can occur intergroup, or between members of different races and genders. Without thinking too hard you can probably cite times in your life when marginalization has occurred in one way or another. Not long ago, I was told of an obvious case of marginalization by a friend in law enforcement.

I had a female friend, let's call her Pepper, who worked in a state law enforcement agency as a detective. Pepper had worked for her agency for only a few years but had transferred into the role from a large municipal police department. Pepper had spent fifteen years at the municipal police department and had obtained mastery over many skills such as defensive tactics, investigation, serving as a field training officer, and more. Even with only a few years at the state law enforcement agency her experience was next to none, and Pepper had already gained recognition for her contributions.

One day, Pepper was talking with a colleague about an upcoming supervisor examination. Those who take the exam are put on a list that allows them to be qualified for promotion based on their performance and seniority.

As Pepper was talking to her colleague with the intent of convincing him to take the exam, her colleague pivoted the conversation, putting emphasis on Pepper instead. Having never considered the possibility, Pepper started to listen and take interest, feeling her excitement at the potential opportunity rise. During that part of the conversation, a male supervisor walked by and injected himself into their conversation. He took the opposite stance and was not supporting the notion that Pepper should take the test and instead listed several reasons why Pepper wouldn't be qualified should she be interested.

The experience that had originally been positive and supportive changed when the supervisor inserted himself into the conversation and provided his unsolicited thoughts. Once the conversation ended and everyone parted ways, Pepper was deflated and had been thoroughly convinced not to take the exam. Unfortunately, that test is only given once every two years, and Pepper missed out on an opportunity that set her career back for years.

All too often people are taught to be humble with their experience, knowledge, and education. We're taught that it's always better to be a team player. Growing up we all hear idioms like "don't rock the boat," "it's better to be seen than heard," or "there's no 'I' in team," and so on.

I'm sure you can come up with some of your own idioms, but at the heart of some like the ones I listed, there is self-sacrifice. A person ends up giving something up, so they don't disturb a "stable" situation, so they're present but not drawing attention or are putting the needs of others first while sacrificing their own.

This is what I call "accepted marginalization" — when people believe the imposed limits society has placed on them given the alternatives. Please note that I didn't say "acceptable" marginalization. There's no excuse for marginalization of any kind. By "accepted," I'm referring to personal acceptance by the person being marginalized.

Let's revisit the story about Pepper to help identify the phenomenon, with the aid of a chart to break down the key points.

Story Breakdown

I included the chart on the next page for a breakdown of the five factors of Pepper's story that are the most important. Law enforcement is a field that is dominated by men, and women represent the minority. This makes it difficult for women to have similar allies or role models for their career. The state agency Pepper worked for was more interested in supporting and promoting those individuals who grew up in their agency and tended to devalue the experience others brought in regard-less of the tenure elsewhere.

Pepper had just enough experience within the agency to qualify for the examination and more than enough when you consider her external experience. However, as mentioned previously, the agency had an affinity for state agency em-ployees grown from within over transfers.

Factors	Phenomenon	Impact on Pepper
Law Enforcement	Male-dominated	Being a female puts her in the minority
State Agency	Average supervisor has less than fifteen years of experience without outside experience, and they have an affinity for those who grow their career within their agency	Makes her experience intimidating to others and makes her an outsider
Years of Experience	Meets the bare minimum number of years with the State Agency to qualify for the exam	In the agency's eyes, she was "barely" qualified, but when combined with her other experience she was overqualified
Supervisor Injection	Law enforcement is extremely hierarchical, and there is a deference to authority	Hadn't considered the test until her friend supported her but then was deflated by a male authority figure
No Test	Tests are only given once every two years	Her career was set back for years

When Pepper's supervisor interjected, he leaned heavily on the fact that she barely met the minimum, even though her combined experience was more than that of the supervisor and was more specialized. He shared his opinion of how ill-prepared Pepper was because she didn't know the agency enough from his perspective, and that the chain of command would likely bypass her anyway because in their eyes she hadn't accrued enough tenure within the agency.

In the end, Pepper deferred to her supervisor because she didn't want to "rock the boat," but her career was set back for years. I found out about the situation many months after the opportunity to test had passed. Knowing she was more than qualified for the opportunity, I asked Pepper how she really felt about the situation.

Pepper admitted that she still felt like she was new and didn't want to stir the pot. Pepper tried to downplay the situation by saying that she hadn't really wanted to take the test and, "only considered it when her friend suggested it." The most disturbing part was when she explained:

> "I felt embarrassed that the supervisor demeaned my experience, and what made it worse was my friend heard all of it. Ultimately, he was the supervisor, and I had to accept what he was telling me. It made sense at the time, but mostly I wanted the conversation to be over because I had set out to support my friend, who supported me and wanted me to test, but was totally deflated by my supervisor."

This is accepted marginalization at its core. Pepper was in a male-dominated field, wasn't respected, and was marginalized for the experience she brought to the table. When an authority figure discredited her qualifications to take the test, even though Pepper felt she was in fact qualified, she accepted the judgment.

Looking back, Pepper knows the supervisor was wrong, and it was her choice to not take the test, but she had been so convinced it wasn't the right thing to do that she missed her chance and set her career back. The sad part is Pepper ended up leaving the agency a year later because she continued to feel that her contributions, ideas, and expertise were marginalized.

There are a variety of critical discourses on race and gender that go in detail on the impacts that oppression has on different groups of individuals throughout history. What I don't believe is discussed enough is the impact on the mindset of individuals who feel they must accept their marginalization. There's a saying that goes, "It's not about the cards you're dealt, but how you play the hand." What happens when society has constantly told you that you can't even play the game? At some point you start to believe it.

If my supervisor says that I'm not ready for a promotion because I haven't been with the agency long enough, they must be right. If I've applied for multiple jobs as a salesperson but am told I'm too young or don't have enough experience, they must be right. If society says I should always have money in savings and a 401k but not bitcoin or NFTs, they must be right. If my boss says that having a child and taking time away will damage my career, they must be right.

I think it's easy enough to understand that at some point we all start to believe the imposed limits society has placed on us. What ends up happening is the cycle of imposed limits starts to become self-perpetuated. We start to internalize every "no" and limit forcing us into the margins, and we accept them and worse yet, end up creating some of our own.

To lead with CARE, you must be ready to recognize this phenomenon and name it to help break that cycle. Maybe there are limits someone in your life or career imposed on you which you've accepted for truth because they were a person of authority.

In the workplace we hear all the time from a manager,

"You know I really like this idea/proposal and will support you 100 percent, but [insert senior manager name] really won't go for this, so I suggest we hold off for now."

I know I've had that happen to me! I understand we can't all run around every day doing everything our hearts desire, but I do believe people are having their hopes, dreams, and aspirations crushed because of accepted marginalization. The purest examples of systemic accepted marginalization can be seen in what I call GAG environments.

Glass Ceiling and Glass Cliff (GAG) Environments

To reach maximum effectiveness as a successful corporate leader and to have concern for all employees, you must learn to be comfortable with the uncomfortable. Like I've mentioned many times now, leadership is a SURE thing, and with that comes opportunities for you to make a difference in someone's career.

Easily identified by DEI initiatives, requiring equitable resolutions, are exclusionary practices leading to accepted marginalization that are embedded in many industries. The two most prominent exclusionary practices that garner attention are glass ceiling and glass cliff (**GAG**) environments. I understand that some may look at this acronym as being too on the nose, but I think that's exactly the point. Both environments create barriers and/or circumstances that limit marginalized groups from achieving optimum success.

Depending on the environment, by marginalized groups I'm talking about those individuals who aren't in the majority or from a preferred social construct. This can mean not being from a particular race, having a specific socioeconomic status, education, or even employment background.

The term glass ceiling speaks to the unofficial, but very real, barriers for career advancement primarily impacting women and other marginalized groups. Think back to the example I used of Pepper being marginalized in a law enforcement agency. In glass ceiling environments, you'll notice affinity biases for certain races, genders, or other socially preferred constructs. The reason it's called glass ceiling is because there exists an invisible, therefore unofficial, barrier for those who aren't part of the majority or from a preferred social construct.

Without concerted efforts to remove said invisible barriers, there will always remain a portion of an organization's population left polarized with little motivation and accepting of their marginalization.

Like glass ceiling, glass cliff environments are those that allow women and other marginalized group members to ascend into senior level positions but only in the most treacherous of times with the highest percentage of failure. This thereby creates a fragile cliff with the expectation that those in the minority will fail, perpetuating a cycle of women and marginalized groups remaining at lower levels of the organization. Both environments serve as methods to silence women and members of marginalized groups, leaving them disenchanted and unmotivated.

As a successful corporate leader, it's your responsibility to remove the GAG from your operating environments, promoting the highest level of diversity, equity, and inclusion.

The best way to promote others and provide opportunity is being a champion for DEI initiatives and an **ACE** at breaking down barriers:

ACKNOWLEDGE INEQUITY
CHANGE INTERACTIONS
EMBRACE DIVERSITY

Acknowledge Inequity

I spoke about getting comfortable with the uncomfortable. If you notice there's inequity in your organization, be willing to acknowledge inequity. I'm not saying you need to be a squeaky wheel, stand outside your building to protest, or be ready to call out your senior leaders. However, there will be times when you witness bias happening in your organization that will lend itself to becoming a GAG environment.

You must have the courage to appropriately — and strategically — acknowledge those circumstances with your leaders because if you notice it, you can be guaranteed that other people in your own organization will also notice it. It will only be a matter of time before one of your employees brings up the matter with you.

Be ready to thoughtfully acknowledge inequity in a way that's hopeful without making commitments that are outside of your capabilities. Many companies are actively making efforts to reduce and eliminate GAG environments, and this is promising. But real change takes time. You need to be a successful corporate leader with a concerning mindset willing to acknowledge that some people have experienced inequities in their careers and will need you as their advocate to enable maximum impactful performance.

Change Interactions

Even if you can't make large scale changes and improve equity, you do have the power to change interactions within the scope of your department and team. Allyship is a great way to change interactions to combat GAG environments. Allyship is a practice where one person in a position of influence can take meaningful action to support another. This has nothing to do with a position of "power."

I've been in several project meetings with men representing the majority and women the minority. In one example, I had a project manager who was a woman, I'll call her Gwen, working with me as a peer on a construction build. Gwen was the lead on the project, but if she posed a question or had the answer to a question, then the other men in the room directed their responses to me. I was Gwen's peer and her responsibilities differed from mine, but regardless of having a different focus others continued to direct the conversation at me.

I had to interrupt the meeting and ask that the other men in the room direct their comments to the Gwen. The men were taken aback but finally started to engage with Gwen. Once the engagement pivoted, Gwen was able to finish the meeting with dedicated focus on her ideas, questions, and recommendations.

After the meeting, I stayed back to talk to Gwen and apologized for how the meeting started off. Gwen was immensely grateful that I changed the interaction but, disturbingly, she admitted it wasn't the first time other men did not actively engage with her even as the lead project manager.

To lead with CARE, you need to be ready and willing to change interactions when you can support another. Otherwise, you're perpetuating a cycle that creates a GAG environment.

Embrace Diversity

I've been very fortunate to have operated in multiple corporate environments that have illuminated the value of embracing diversity. Coming from a law enforcement background, tradition was ingrained in me. Everything as inconsequential as how your gig line (the alignment of the seam of a uniform shirt, belt buckle, and uniform trouser flyseam) should look, covering up tattoos, and the inability for men to wear earrings were meticulously outlined and regimented. While they had their purpose, those traditions meant the opposite of diversity.

Those traditions followed me into the corporate environment and forced me to quell my authentic self. It wasn't until I worked for my manager, Mary Jane at Meta (more on Mary Jane in the next chapter) that I realized the value of embracing my authentic self and allowing my diversity to be an advantage.

I relished the experience I had working with Mary Jane and realized that I didn't need to keep my genuine self subdued to be considered professional. While working for Mary Jane, I decided it was time to let my own tattoos show, to put in my earring, and get rid of the gig line. I remember the day I walked into work as my "authentic self." Mary Jane looked at me and said, "About time," smiled, and went back to work.

Diversity can take shape in a variety of fashions, and you must be able to embrace it even if it means no longer repressing your true self or desires. For some it could mean feeling comfortable about starting a family without fear or worry about the impact of their career. By achieving authenticity and embracing diversity, you're opening the doors for your employees to bring their entire selves into the workplace without fear of it limiting their career opportunities, paving the way to optimal performance enablement.

A leader can be successful in any environment when they have concern for those that work for them and with them, are authentic in their approach, realistic with their own capabilities and in the capabilities of others, and empathetic toward others.

How you interact with your staff is heavily influenced by the company and organizations culture. The bedrock of culture is built on a foundation of good ethical behavior and an environment rich in diversity, equity, and inclusion.

You need to always be concerned for the employees whom you are entrusted with as your charge. Utilizing some of the skills I introduced in this section like DREAM and TACK will put you in a position to help break the cycle of GAG environments and become an ACE at breaking down barriers. While it's not always easy to do, keeping a pulse on how your employees are doing will ensure they're operating at their full potential and will make your job a whole lot easier.

Key Takeaways

1	Often the most obvious area of unethical behavior, department ethics is where most employees will experience strife within their immediate working relationships. Due to the close working relationships employees have within their department, department ethics often has the greatest impact on culture.
2	Leadership ethics specifically relates to the ethics an individual leader operates by. Any time you're put in a position of trust and are responsible for leading others, how you respond in those positions is a measure of your leadership ethics.
3	A successful corporate leader can act ethically by following the **DREAM**: direct, transparent communication, role modeling, equitable decision-making, allyship, and managing with integrity.
4	**ADD** authenticity when it comes to exercising DEI in the workplace: accept everyone, don't fake it, and do be present.
5	Marginalization is a social construct where a person, group, idea, or their actions and contributions are rendered powerless and insignificant. As a successful corporate leader, you must be ready to help break the cycle of internalized and accepted marginalization.

Be Authentic:
Leadership Styles

If I had to pick a favorite concept within **CARE**, it's authenticity. Ironically, even though it's my favorite, it took the longest to be good at. Early in my career, I was a sponge. Especially when I shifted from the public to the private sector. I didn't understand what true leadership in the workplace looked like. What I did know was what my Tata, a nickname for my grandfather, instilled in me while he helped raise me, and that is you always put your family first.

This value bled over into the workplace because I look at those who are in my company and department as my family. Placing the needs of others before my own is how CARE came to be, but the problem is that if you don't know who you are as a person, or a leader, then it's hard to understand how to help others.

That's the conundrum with authenticity. You can't fake it until you make it. You need to ground yourself in your values and start by knowing wholeheartedly who you are as a person to be an effective leader. If a successful corporate leader is highly invested in others, as they should be, then they can lose perspective on who they really are if they aren't grounded.

This is a bad thing if you start to adapt to your surroundings by way of assimilation and doing what others are doing for the sake of ease without knowing how to be true to yourself. If you're in a toxic environment, that type of assimilation can be detrimental to you and your employees.

Many leaders fail to realize the importance of understanding and adapting their own leadership style and instead do what they think people expect them to do, and that can lead to disastrous outcomes.

Let's look at two examples of leadership styles. I once worked for a leader, I'll call him Adam, who had the worst leadership style I've ever witnessed and been subjected to. Adam was a "textbook" corporate leader. He had an impressive resume having graduated from an Ivy League college and spent a short time working for a government agency. Charming and charismatic, Adam commanded attention and was able to easily gain respect from those who listened.

On the surface, Adam had all the "qualities" to be a good leader. The problem is that outside of the public view, Adam did nothing to help those around him. Instead, with a draconian style of leadership, he used everyone around him to their most extreme limits, constantly pushing harder and harder, asking for more without giving support or guidance. When he was done getting all he could out of a person, Adam either had them replaced or layered them away within the organization.

One of the worst behaviors I witnessed was Adam completely demeaning one my direct reports on a phone call to the point where they were crying. The whole situation was awkward because of how callous Adam was in his approach and the way he twisted facts in the conversation to meet his ultimate purpose of getting the employee to remove themselves from their position.

The time I spent working for Adam was hard. While he was good at outward displays of leadership, particularly when working with senior stakeholders, as an employee on his team, I realized I would never thrive under such a leader. Eventually

I was able to escape the situation, and I was fortunate to find a leader who opened my eyes to another style of leadership.

I found myself working for one of the best leaders in my whole career. Mary Jane was the epitome of what it means to be an authentic leader. I won't do her any justice with a description, but I'll do my best because understanding what she looks like is key to recognizing her authenticity. Mary Jane was about 5'5", had a quiet demeanor, athletic with a thin build, with long black hair to her waist, and walked with poise, ready to attack with the speed of a viper. Most surprising of all, both of her arms were covered in full sleeve tattoos.

She could easily navigate even the toughest of management environments. The team had an affectionate nickname that was only partially correct, referring to Mary Jane as a "bull in a China shop." The saying was accurate in the sense that she wasn't afraid to enter a situation and take control, even if it meant hurting feelings and ignoring protocol to get the job done.

However, she didn't do anything without methodical and intentional thought and behavior. Mary Jane was one of the brightest leaders I worked for, and she could lead an organization to meet objectives like no other — she did so without sucking the spirit out of them.

Best of all, she cared about every single person in her organization, all the way down to the hourly worker. She didn't coddle anyone, but she was authentic in her concern for others. If there was inclement weather, you better believe Mary Jane was out on foot checking on every single person. If anyone was ever being mistreated, there would be hell to pay. I was always blown away by Mary Jane — never afraid of what others may think about her and always demonstrating CARE for others even in the toughest situations, Mary Jane was the epitome of the authentic leadership style.

Working for Mary Jane opened my eyes to the possibilities of being able to be myself in the work environment without worrying about what others think, while still putting the needs of others before my own. What was especially shocking is that while Mary Jane and I would interact in a specific manner and had our unique working relationship, she could quickly adapt her style, so it would resonate with others.

Therein lies the key to being authentic. Once you're grounded in yourself and know the type of leader you are, you shouldn't be afraid to adapt your style to better communicate with your team when needed. Different styles will work for different leaders, and they may need to modify for specific direct reports. It doesn't mean you're any less effective. In fact, a manager who can adapt their style to meet a specific direct report's needs is operating on a whole new level of leadership if they remain authentic in their approach.

As you read *Lead with CARE*, I know you're looking to develop your leadership skills. I applaud you for investing time in yourself. Leadership and management principles continue to evolve as more and more research becomes available. Without giving regular attention to addressing your needs, your abilities as a successful corporate leader could be left by the wayside.

To help arm you with skills for identifying your authenticity and to provide tips for adapting to leadership challenges in the workplace, I'll present some common leadership styles, introduce some emerging trends, and highlight some common leadership pitfalls to avoid.

Chapter 6: Common Leadership Styles

Now that you're well entrenched in your desire to be a leader, **SURE** you're ready for people management, and committed to exercising vulnerability with **TAPE** all while breaking down barriers like an **ACE**, let's talk about leadership styles.

Before I really understood what true leadership should look like, I knew I loved being in the thick of things. Early in my management career at Apple, I was introduced to leadership concepts, but it wasn't until the doctorate program at USC that I studied multiple leadership styles.

Through my studies I was able to identify elements of my natural abilities that aligned with research-based leadership styles. While the experience was illuminating for me, you don't need to identify with only a single style to be a successful corporate leader. Quite frankly, you may find one style that serves as your "definitive" style, but having the ability to adjust on the fly will serve you well.

The following information will provide you with a shortcut to understand some leadership styles empirical research has identified and to perhaps spark your curiosity to learn more on your own. I do believe there's a lot of value in grounding yourself in one style that suits you. Some styles don't work well in certain environments. If you operate a certain way as a successful corporate leader, you may determine that you have no place in certain careers because your style would be counterproductive.

There's no shortage of leadership concepts and styles out there. The list I present are ones from my experience that I've either embraced or have witnessed in others. This list is meant to shed some light on what you may find on your journey:

- **Transformational**
- **Transactional**
- **Authentic**
- **Servant**
- **Adaptive**

Transformational Leadership

Transformational leadership focuses on how leaders invest in their employees, bringing about their full potential, to influence behavior. The essence of transformational leadership is creating a connection with employees, so you can improve motivation and morale. While this leadership style sounds straightforward enough, it's quite complex. It closely mirrors a transactional leadership style, which I will go into detail next, that prioritizes accomplishments over authenticity. Transformational leadership shines if you have a leader with a high level of charisma who's inspired to invest in others, embraces authenticity, and has a healthy appetite for risk taking.

There are four distinct factors that define transformational leadership.

1. **Inspirational motivation** — Leveraging the idealized influence a leader has with their team members, a leader with inspirational motivation can supercharge their staff with inspirational mantras and speeches. Through the appropriate use of transparent and frequent communication, these leaders can communicate a high level of expectations to followers while also showing support to meet those expectations, leaving people with a sense of purpose, and motivated to not let their leader down.

2. **Intellectual stimulation** — This leadership factor describes a leader's ability to inspire others to think outside the box and challenge the status quo. Not to the point of dissension, leaders with intellectual stimulation encourage others to try something new even if it means failure. By creating a safe space for experimentation, intellectual stimulation creates psychological safety for followers.

3. **Individualized consideration** — Knowing that everyone has their unique circumstances, individualized consideration creates space for leaders to understand their team members personally. As an ultimate way of expressing concern, leaders won't take a one-size-fits-all approach to managing people in their organization.

Benefits of Transformational Leadership

The four factors of transformational leadership paint a picture of what it means to adapt, or "transform," the expected outcomes of a leader's team members. Employees following this type of leader will tend to have a higher level of intrinsic motivation, or personal investment, especially when they can identify with a leader's values and are therefore highly invested in meeting the company/department goals. Due to the space for intellectual stimulation, there's also an argument that this leadership style will inspire a higher level of innovation within teams. For a leader who can naturally identify with the four factors, this type of leadership style can be very authentic. If charisma is a natural trait, transformational leaders may find it easy to inspire, motivate, and show concern for others.

Development of Transformational Leadership

You need to be a strong role model for your team to have success as a transformational leader. With immutable morals and values, leaders of this style are predictable and consistent in the eyes of others. Sometimes a daunting task, transformational leaders are always communicating their vision and are highly effective at gaining stakeholder buy-in. The goal of the transformational leader is to inspire others to follow, so impactful output on a team is optimized and company/department goals are constantly met.

Drawbacks of Transformational Leadership

It's easy to understand the definition of the four factors, but it's hard to provide definitive clarity on how to achieve them. For example, there's no one characteristic that defines a high moral character. There is also no one precise way to communicate a vision to ensure buy-in or alignment. The only real way to determine whether transformational leadership is effective is through anecdotal record. Due to the high level of charisma more transformational leaders exhibit, there can be an opportunity to abuse the relationship, leading to more of a transactional leadership outcome.

Regardless of some of the drawbacks, transformational leadership provides a strong basis for demonstrating concern, authenticity, and empathy for others.

Transactional Leadership

Transactional leadership is the fancy definition for the most common leadership style everyone is familiar with: the leader-follower (or manager-employee) binary. Transactions within the binary occur on a regular basis. For instance, if an employee performs well enough, the manager may decide it's time for a raise. Conversely, if the employee fails to arrive at work on time, the manager may issue discipline. On the surface, this type of leadership style doesn't create trust. Unlike transformational leadership, transactional leadership does not require a leader to necessarily be of high moral character, and they're interested in achievements over authenticity.

There are two distinct factors associated with transactional leadership:

1. **Contingent reward —** Easy-to-understand, contingent reward answers the question, "What's in it for me?" Based on the accomplishment of a follower, they're granted a specific reward contingent on meeting an outcome. If a sales department has a specific sales target and they hit that target, they'll be granted the reward that's contingent on accomplishing the task.

2. **Management by exception —** Often seen as "micromanaging," management by exception involves active or passive corrective action by a leader. If an employee arrives late to work, active management by exception would occur on the spot, addressing the tardiness as soon as the employee finally arrives. Basically, it's a manager immediately acting and addressing something wrong. An example of passive corrective action would be a manager providing a poor performance evaluation if an employee didn't meet a sales quota at the end of the year.

Benefits of Transactional Leadership

Transactional leadership represents your down-and-dirty style of traditional leadership. It's not reliant on having any one personality trait or specific quality. Instead, it's a straightforward approach to setting and meeting outcomes. Especially beneficial in a task-heavy environment like sales or customer service, if responsibilities are communicated at the outset, it's a simple style to learn and implement. It's also well suited for employees who are extrinsically motivated by self-interest, like monetary reward, to get the job done.

Development of Transactional Leadership

This style is easy to put into place. I look at this method of leadership as the "default mode." Everyone gets exposed to this in their life. A parent or adult figure who told you to do all your homework before allowing you to hang out with friends, watch, or play on your phone was a transactional leader. The only part of this style that takes some effort is understanding how to communicate expected outcomes and using active or passive corrective action at the right time. You don't want to be seen as micromanaging when attempting to actively correct behavior.

Drawbacks of Transactional Leadership

Since this style doesn't require any one personality trait or specific quality, this style of leadership can be very impersonal. You can have a leader who isn't invested in their employees, cares more about the job getting done, and uses employees like resources, exhausting them as needed to meet a goal. You may have employees who are so self-interested in achieving their contingent reward, they'll do anything to meet that goal, even if it means ruining stakeholder relationships to get there. Worse yet, you could have both a leader who doesn't care about employees and employees who don't care about anyone but themselves. Transactional leadership isn't a favorable style where there's a need to play the "long game" and a necessity for company/department or employee development.

Authentic Leadership

Authentic leadership is a leadership style that has a foundation based on strong morals, is genuine in its approach, and demonstrates empathy. Led by a sense of purpose, authentic leaders have strong values, focus on developing trusted relationships, always adhere to their values, and show empathy toward others. An important aspect of authentic leadership is that leaders who adhere to this style are deeply passionate about the work they do. An authentic leader will be at the center of it all, no matter if it's a specific cause or it's nurturing others in the department. Admirably, an authentic leader will never allow their values to be compromised regardless of the circumstances.

There are four components that are associated with authentic leadership:

1. **Self-awareness —** Not allowing themselves to be pulled away from their "true north," authentic leaders constantly reflect on their positionality to understand and assess their motives, goals, and values. Leaders of this style have a high degree of emotional intelligence.

2. **Internalized moral perspective —** As part of being self-aware, authentic leaders will make decisions based on their internal moral perspective. Not allowing outside influences like societal or peer pressure to influence their decisions, authentic leaders can be depended on for their decision making because choices are based on their values and purpose.

3. **Balanced processing —** Similar to having an internal moral perspective, authentic leaders process information in an objective way. Able to accept the opinions of others and consider counter narratives, authentic leaders maintain balanced decision making free of bias and open to other perspectives.

4. **Relational transparency —** An essential element to providing clear transparent communication, authentic leaders consider their relationships with others when communicating openly. This doesn't mean communicating everything, but instead it means an authentic leader isn't afraid to be transparent with the good and bad sides of their personality.

Benefits of Authentic Leadership

With a person who operates with an authentic leadership style, you know what you're going to get all the time. Since they operate with such a high reverence for adhering to their value structure when making decisions or dealing with others, there's no guesswork on what to expect. Best of all, authentic leaders have a genuine way of developing trusted relationships and maintaining those relationships over time. Particularly valuable in industries that are unpredictable, followers appreciate the dependability and reliability an authentic leader brings to the organization.

Development of Authentic Leadership

This leadership style is one of the hardest to develop. Being a strong authentic leader requires one to be always grounded in their values with a high level of self-awareness. An internalized moral perspective with an unwavering decision-making process takes knowledge and experience to develop. It's not enough to have a high value system. Those interested in an authentic leadership style need to survive the "test of time," allowing them to be in the harshest of leadership environments and successfully making decisions unhampered by outside influence.

Drawbacks of Authentic Leadership

While the style itself has a lot to offer, getting to the point of being an effective, authentic leader takes a lot of time. There's no magic number that says a person has enough years of experience, knowledge, or training to be considered an authentic leader. You only know a person has "enough" experience when they can make unwavering decisions regardless of outside influence. Additionally, there's no finite measure to say a person's value system is good enough.

Instead, only time can determine if a person can be considered an authentic leader based on the totality of their contributions.

Servant Leadership

Servant leadership makes the needs of their team members a priority above all else, especially for those team members who have been socially marginalized. This type of leadership style can tend to be at odds with traditional concepts. It can be perplexing for some that a leader can focus on empowering others and make their team members a priority to achieve company/department goals, but when team members benefit from being empowered, invested in, and developed by an influential leader, they become impactful contributors toward meeting company/department targets.

For servant leadership to be effective, team members can't fear bringing their entire self to the company/department. Without being able to be their natural selves, flaws included, a servant leader would have difficulty developing areas of improvement and the team members wouldn't fully benefit from the activities of the servant leader. Once team members start benefiting from the investment, the company/department should see performance improvements resonate throughout.

There are seven servant leader behaviors that are essential to the style:

1. **Conceptualize** — A leader needs to know their operating environment and organization thoroughly. Conceptualizing will allow the leader to predict organizational outcomes and identify when things are going wrong. Doing so will allow the leader to position their team members in the best opportunities to leverage their talents.

2. **Emotional healing** — Like expressing empathy, servant leaders will remain sensitive to the needs of others and be prepared to respond accordingly. Even if

it means only providing an ear to listen, servant leaders are always ready to be present.

3. **Putt team members first** — This is the core behavior of servant leadership. Servant leaders put the needs of others before their own.

4. **Help team members grow and succeed** — Team members must trust the leader enough to bring their whole self to the organization. In that way, a servant leader can identify the development a team member needs so growth can be fostered, enabling them to reach new levels of success.

5. **Behave ethically** — Similar to having the solid morals associated with authentic leadership, a servant leader does what is right, when it's right. This is especially important in the eyes of their team members. A servant leader needs to back up talk with action.

6. **Empowerment** — As team members develop their skill sets, under the servant leader's guidance the leader needs to be able to stand back at the right time and allow their team members to perform. This is where the value of conceptualization rings true. If a servant leader maintains a pulse on the organization, they will be able to allow their team members to control how they leverage their talents in the best opportunities.

7. **Create value for the community** — The pur-pose that drives a servant leader is the ability to share their skills with others, giving back to those who need a helping hand, and elevating those around them to new levels.

Benefits of Servant Leadership

Perhaps the biggest benefit of servant leadership is its potential for long-term impact on team members. We discussed that it's slightly counterintuitive to believe such a heavy investment in others could have a sustainable impact. However, it's true that those on the receiving end of servant leadership improve performance and by default improve the performance of the entire organization. Best of all, studies have shown that the investment from servant leaders creates a positive effect for team members in other areas of their lives.

Development of Servant Leadership

Servant leadership works best for those with an altruistic motivation and purpose to help others. This leadership style won't work for leaders who only seek to invest in others for personal gain. While servant leadership is not entirely selfless because the servant leader should feel rewarded when investing in others, the outcome should not be self-serving. As such, to start developing a servant leadership style a leader needs to practice the seven behaviors listed above, starting with putting team members first in all things. Once successfully and consistently accomplished, the leader can start working on conceptualizing and emotional healing. The other traits should start to fall into place relatively easy. Servant leadership is a concrete example of being a SURE thing, and implementing the seven behaviors will take time to get right.

Drawbacks of Servant Leadership

The obvious drawback is the inconsistency brought on by the name itself. There's a paradox of being a leader while being a servant. In that sense, by pure definition some people are put off right from the start. There can also be confusion about the benefits to the company/department. The by-product of servant leadership is that the company/department will benefit from the increased skill of the employees of the servant leader. The difficulty is clearly targeting specific company/department improvements if the purpose of the servant leader is to target employee betterment, not organizational goals.

Adaptive Leadership

Adaptive leadership focuses on helping empower employees with the skills to adapt to the multitude of obstacles they face in the workplace. This leadership style is different from the others because it's less about the leader's skill and characteristics and more about improving the skills of employees, so they can help themselves.

The adaptive leadership style resonates with me the most because it categorizes situational challenges employees may face and recommends different approaches to remedy each.

Particularly valuable are six specific leadership behaviors a leader can perform to better prepare employees to handle and overcome unforeseen obstacles in the workplace. Of all the leadership styles I introduce, this style highly emphasizes preparing employees to handle the obscure social environment they'll encounter in the workplace.

There are six adaptive leadership behaviors that are essential for a leader to implement with this style:

1. **Get on the balcony** — Like getting on a highest point possible, or maintaining a 30,000-foot view, this can be thought of as a leader having the "big picture" or, as I like to say, "having a pulse on the organization." Getting on the balcony requires a leader to know the goings-on of the organization. This is achieved by developing focus groups as advisors, holding regular organizational meetings, or popping into meetings purely as an observer.

2. **Identify the adaptive challenge** — There are three primary challenges employees face in the workplace. They're technical, adaptive, or a combination of the two. Technical challenges are clearly defined and can

be solved with "hard skills." Adaptive challenges aren't straightforward and don't have easy answers. Technical and adaptive challenges are those that have a clear challenge but no clear solution. The key is to be able to identify the appropriate adaptive challenge an employee is facing.

3. **Regulate distress** — Identify when employees are reaching their maximum ability to tolerate stress and helping them regulate that stress. Five key behaviors that help in regulating distress are providing direction, protection, orientation, conflict management, and establishing productive norms.

4. **Maintain disciplined attention** — A leader helps their employees face their challenges head on by offering encouragement and support. An important element to maintaining disciplined attention is calling out the "elephant in the room" if employees aren't willing to speak up about their challenges.

5. **Give the work back to the people** — It's important to understand that adaptive leadership does not mean "rescuing" employees from their challenges. You are ready to respond to employees in need and arm them with skills to overcome their obstacles but need to get out of the way and let them get the job done.

6. **Protect leadership voices from below** — Everyone in the organization needs to feel like they have a voice. An adaptive leader ensures that everyone — even the most junior person, particularly historically marginalized individuals — feels like their opinions, thoughts, and comments matter just as much as everyone else's.

Benefits of Adaptive Leadership

This leadership style's employee focus bolsters its effectiveness. Rather than the leader being at the epicenter of change, the leader practices behaviors that will bring the best out of their employees. This process requires heavy employee engagement for a leader to respond at the right moment with appropriate support to keep an employee from faltering. Additionally, there are specific leader behaviors like regulating distress and maintaining disciplined attention that, once mastered by an employee, will grant them abilities they can use throughout their career.

Development of Adaptive Leadership

For a leader to be effective in adaptive leadership, they must have the knowledge and ability to recognize and differentiate between technical, adaptive, and technical/adaptive challenges. Each requires specific solutions, and if a leader helps an employee approach a situation or implement a solution that isn't appropriate given the specific challenge, they'll be destined to fail. An adaptive leader must get comfortable with being hands off when an employee faces a challenge, because they're not there to rescue. Instead, they're guiding employees to solutions while providing them with the skills to overcome obstacles on their own.

Drawbacks of Adaptive Leadership

This leadership style is highly technical and complex. From being able to correctly identify the problem at hand, to responding with the appropriate leadership behavior without stepping into rescue, it's a lot to handle. The complexity brings with it many opportunities for error. This style is best suited for leaders who are highly specialized and experts by their own right in their field. In that sense, they're more likely to steer employees in the right direction because they will have mastered the ability to diagnose challenges and be more willing to step back and allow employees to solve situations on their own.

Leadership styles may evolve as you grow as a leader and morph according to the environment you find yourself working in. You'll find that some leadership styles are more effective than others depending on the industry. Ultimately, there's no single perfect style that works for everyone everywhere, so don't get caught up in the details. Research different styles if it's of interest to you.

Key Takeaways

1	Transformational leaders create a connection with employees so they can improve motivation and create a safe space for experimentation. These leaders can influence others because of their moral character and high level of charisma.
2	Transactional leadership follows the leader-follower (or manager-employee) binary. When an employee accomplishes a desired outcome, they can be rewarded — but reward is contingent on that outcome. In management by exception, leaders take active or passive corrective action to address something wrong.
3	Authentic leaders have strong morals, are genuine in their approach, and demonstrate empathy. They're led by a sense of purpose, have strong values, focus on developing trusted relationships, and are dependable and reliable. Since they operate with such a high reverence for adhering to their value structure when making decisions or in dealing with others, there's no guesswork on what to expect.
4	Servant leaders make the needs of employees a priority above all else, especially for those employees who have been socially marginalized. This type of leadership style can tend to be at odds with traditional concepts. When team members benefit from being empowered, invested in, and developed by an influential leader, they will become impactful contributors toward meeting company/department targets.
5	Adaptive leaders focus on helping to empower employees with the skills to adapt to the multitude of obstacles they face in the workplace. This style is less about the leader's skill and characteristics and more about improving the skills of employees so they can help themselves.

Chapter 7: Workplace Emerging Trends

There isn't one perfect leadership style. Given the many variables associated with leading people, several contributing factors can impact how you respond to employees, and vice versa. It's important to note a leader's style (or styles) is developed based out of a purely social construction — affected by the totality of their lived experiences inside and outside of the workplace and based on societal influence.

How others behave in social environments is dictated by the masses. Based on the social context, the masses also dictate what can be considered good or bad behavior based on what's accepted by the majority. Global trends can play a factor in shifting social opinion about acceptable behavior. Think about how COVID-19 played a part in shifting social acceptance of work from home for employees. There are now very strong considerations in favor of work from home where previous considerations were dismissed as employees being entitled or lazy.

The never-ending change that accompanies social opinion means that you should always be aware of emerging trends. When operating with **CARE**, the only way to remain nimble and adaptable is to stay abreast of what's on the horizon. Three emerging trends you should consider and watch for include: inclusive leadership, accountability, and well-being.

Inclusive Leadership

Inspired by the societal push for diversity, equity, and inclusion (DEI), inclusive leadership seeks to improve a sense of belonging for members of an organization. By improving a shared identity, reducing status differences, and enhancing employee engagement, inclusive leadership seeks to dismantle historical barriers that previously hindered effective DEI efforts.

You'll start seeing more companies put measures in place that pave the way for diversity, equity, and inclusion. The amount of societal pressure is too much for the workplace to ignore. At minimum, you need to understand the principles that make them effective and inclusive to lead with CARE. One step beyond that, you should adapt some of the practices. Principles of creating a shared identity, minimizing status differences, and improving involvement of those who've been historically marginalized are essential to inclusive leaders.

Accountability

Whether it's because of a generational gap or the Fourth Industrial Revolution, the blurring separation between the digital and physical world that has separated people from the consequences associated with interpersonal interaction, there's a trending lack of appropriate accountability.

It could be the result of the prolific use of social media where users interact with the outside world one dimensionally, and comments, judgements, and reactions aren't recognized in the same immediate transactional process associated with face-to-face communication. It could also be the result of the increased use of video conferencing across mediums like FaceTime, Zoom, or Google Meet, where essential nonverbal cues are harder to notice.

Whatever the cause, the need to improve accountability within the manager-employee binary is on the rise. You need to operate with a growth mindset, adapting new techniques (like those introduced in *Lead with CARE*) that are meant to hold yourself and your employees accountable for all actions and contributions.

Accountability at its foundation goes beyond finger pointing when things go wrong. Instead, it can be thought of along an ethical dimension in which acts of commission and omission account for appropriate or inappropriate behavior in the workplace. Appropriate accountability mechanisms within the manager-employee binary can improve operational effectiveness within an organization and contribute to career success.

Well-Being

As a category, I look at well-being to include trends that prioritize physiological and psychological health. Grabbing headlines recently are employee desires to work from home. While they're similar, the previous common narrative was an emphasis on work-life balance. Whichever way you look at it, American society is shifting away from sacrificing personal health and family priorities for twelve-hour days in the office, fighting traffic, and missing out on quality time.

COVID-19 played a significant part in this shift because in the eyes of employees, they're just as effective (if not more so) working from home as they were in the office. From the employer's perspective, the battleground of well-being offerings can mean the loss or gain of talented resources. In this war the victor will be determined by the company that can find the right balance of maintaining shareholder and investor profit and making employee well-being mandatory rather than optional.

If a successful corporate leader can't assist their organization in retaining resources by supporting employee well-being, they will be on the losing end of employee retention. This is evident in many news articles and current research surrounding talks of "the great resignation" and "quiet quitting."

Employees who were part of the great resignation prioritized well-being over generous compensation packages.

Employees who are quiet quitting are no longer going the extra mile at work because the rewards aren't worth the self-sacrifice. Instead, more and more employees are putting forth enough effort to meet the minimum of employer expectations but no more. In either case, well-being is the main desire of the workforce.

Finding and identifying with the appropriate leadership style or trend for your personality — allowing you to embrace your authenticity — isn't an easy task. But that's part of the enjoyment of being a successful corporate leader. Your goal shouldn't be to "just get the job done." Instead, when you can successfully and positively influence another person's career, you'll instill genuine gratitude.

Key Takeaways

1	By improving shared identity, reducing status differences, and enhancing employee engagement, inclusive leadership seeks to dismantle historical barriers that previously hindered effective DEI efforts. Societal pressure to move toward inclusivity is too much for the workplace to ignore, so at minimum, you need to understand the principles of inclusive leadership.
2	The need to improve accountability is on the rise, so you'll need to operate with a growth mindset, adapting new techniques meant to hold yourself and your followers accountable for all actions and contributions.
3	Personal well-being is a growing consideration for workers, capable of outweighing even generous compensation packages; American society is shifting away from sacrificing personal health and family priorities for work. If you can't assist your organization in retaining talent by supporting employee well-being, then you'll be on the losing end of employee retention.

Chapter 8: Common Pitfalls to Avoid

By now you should have a few things solidified at the forefront of your mind. Leadership is a **SURE** thing, you can be an **ACE** at promoting and supporting others, and you can be the **DREAM** of ethical leadership. Regardless of the materials or sections you've connected with so far, there could be some alarm bells going off.

Within the complex matrix that is leading others, even with the purest of intentions, there are numerous things that can and will go wrong. See the countless news articles, research publications, and social media posts about companies and leaders failing every day. Learned lessons or actions to prevent future failures can get lost in all the noise. I could write an encyclopedia on all the actions, circumstances, and situations you should avoid.

Conversely, when you provide **CARE** to your company, department, and employees, failures that occur will be recoverable with minimal impact to those around you. In my many years absorbing case studies, working in volatile environments within the corporate tech industry, and mentoring others, I've identified common pitfalls every leader should avoid. By understanding these, you'll be able to ease some misgivings about your role as a successful corporate leader. The four common pitfalls are:

1. **Thinking you won't make mistakes**
2. **Not learning from your mistakes**
3. **Not knowing the difference between a crisis and having a bad day**
4. **Not understanding imposter syndrome**

Common Pitfall #1: Thinking You Won't Make Mistakes

I'm throwing this right out there — being a perfect leader to everyone, everywhere, all the time is a myth. You're going to make mistakes, but you must get over it and move on. Think about the mistakes you went through learning to ride a bike. In the beginning, you're trying to remember everything — maintaining balance, keeping your legs moving, steering, watching where you're going, keeping an eye out for your surroundings, and how to stop. Then over time, the number of things you were mentally processing fell into the background until you only had to focus on one or two things at a time.

However, how many times have you crashed even after learning how to ride a bike? Once you get the basics down, your confidence improves, and maybe you try some tricks and inevitably crash. Maybe you tried to learn how to ride a road bike with "clip in" shoes and inevitably crash. Maybe you get a mountain bike and inevitably crash a lot. Maybe some of you have never learned to ride a bike, let alone crashed one.

Even when we're committed to an activity and have done it for years, mistakes happen. Leadership is no exception. You'll mess up, and sometimes you'll mess up hard, especially when being authentic. Hopefully, with the skills I introduce, you can pick yourself up and dust yourself off, so you can bounce back resiliently. In the end, own up to all your mistakes — because they will happen — and get over it. Tomorrow is a new day.

Common Pitfall #2: Not Learning from Your Mistakes

Some of you may laugh or do a double take at this pitfall. No, I didn't make a mistake. (See what I did there?) I can't count the number of times as a leader when I've witnessed mistakes that caused a disruption and required serious work to remedy, only to have the same thing happen again.

Your time is valuable. You'll be pulled in many different directions all the time, so it's an easy thing to overlook, but you must implement practices that allow you to avoid repeating mistakes, especially mistakes you can prevent. You'll be making mistakes, so you might as well learn from them in the process.

Leaders often don't take advantage of the lessons that can come from assessing their mistakes. Make it part of your mindfulness exercise. I don't mean you should fixate on a mistake. Instead, think back on the mistake to understand how to take ownership of it, and consider what you can do in the future to prevent it from happening again.

I've had several minor epiphanies while practicing mindfulness (more on this in the next chapter), many of which helped me realize I can't allow a mistake to consume me, which I used to do. Instead, mindfulness has allowed me to interpret a situation on a higher level and prevent the mistake from reoccurring.

Common Pitfall #3: Not Knowing the Difference between a Crisis and Having a Bad Day

I once had a classmate who said, when discussing overreactions to a crisis, "Sometimes you just need to know the difference between a crisis and having a bad day." I was able to relate to this statement on so many levels, but especially in leadership. As a leader, you're going to have situations pop up and take you by surprise. Often in moments of uncertainty, mixed with some fear, leaders will immediately start acting as if the sky is falling and their entire team will follow suit. When the dust settles, the leaders realize — but often won't admit — they overreacted. It was only a bad day.

When you have responsibility for others, you need to keep your emotions in check. Inevitably a legitimate crisis will arise, but if you're a leader who constantly cries wolf, your team will become innocuous to your cries and will likely be slow to react until they confirm for themselves. This delay will start a domino effect of failures.

Regardless of whether you're in crisis, remember to exercise thoughtful judgement on a regular basis, so you can practice slowing down when you need to. Would you rather spend one minute gathering your thoughts and corralling your emotions to make the right decision or a potentially infinite number of minutes trying to fix a hastily made poor decision? I already mentioned you'll make mistakes. Taking time to collect yourself during a crisis could reduce the magnitude of the mistake.

Common Pitfall #4: Not Understanding Imposter Syndrome

Mistakes are bad and can ruin a person's day, but as a leader the worst pitfall of all is not knowing what imposter syndrome is. I didn't know what imposter syndrome was until I started at Meta. Once I did learn, it opened my eyes to so many negative outcomes that had happened to me in my career.

Imposter syndrome is feeling like you're a fake, that people around you are going to realize you're a fake, and that you don't deserve to be where you are. All of this goes through a person's head, often without any prompting from their environment. It's a self-defeating thought process that doesn't give bearing to the hard work and effort a person puts in to get where they are. Imposter syndrome can happen to anyone, both you and your employees alike. I experienced a bout of imposter syndrome shortly after joining Meta.

At Meta, new employees are taught about imposter syndrome in orientation because it commonly happens when people change jobs or roles and are faced with new responsibilities in new environments. Still, I didn't really give it any attention because I've always prided myself on being able to remain resilient in even the most difficult of situations.

Nevertheless, there I was six months later with Mary Jane respectfully telling me to "get my head out of my ass." (She didn't use those words exactly, but that's how I translated them, and it worked.) Mary Jane not only reminded me of the imposter syndrome conversation from orientation but also mentioned that when I was experiencing it, six months on the job, was the most common time frame for it to occur. Mary Jane then went on to help quell my negative thoughts by reminding me of the hard work, effort, and education that I acquired, making me a perfect candidate for the job in the first place. It was a great lesson for me and one that I share with others regularly.

As leaders, we aren't infallible, and we will never be perfect all the time, but allowing imposter syndrome to creep in could derail your success completely. Not to mention, we must be constantly supporting our employees and looking for signs of imposter syndrome in them.

You'll often notice deprecating remarks, self-doubt, or uncharacteristic performance for someone experiencing imposter syndrome. I can't cover all the solutions for someone experiencing imposter syndrome here, but I can say the most important skill is to "do be present" (**ADD**). If you aren't present in the moment with your employee, then you could miss some important cues that would help you interpret when and if they're experiencing imposter syndrome.

Tactics to Overcome Common Leadership Challenges

The following leadership skills help with overcoming common pitfalls, and everyone, regardless of style, would benefit from them. When facing uncertainty, and when you find yourself in an inevitable pitfall, there are six tactics I encourage every leader to take to reach new heights like an ALPINE climber.

You can reach the lofty **ALPINE** heights by:

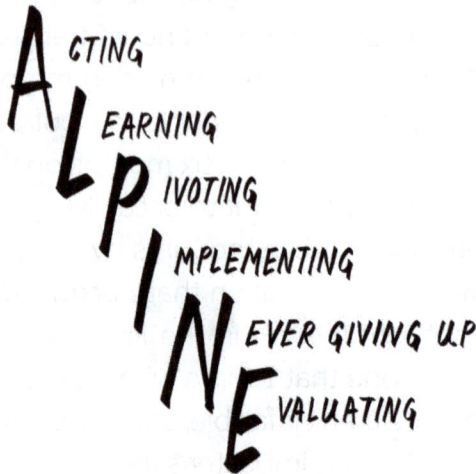

A CTING

L EARNING

P IVOTING

I MPLEMENTING

N EVER GIVING UP

E VALUATING

Acting

Whatever obstacle or mountain of an objective you face, never stop taking action. Taking action does not mean a reckless abandonment or wanton disregard of common sense. While exercising mindfulness in a crisis is extremely useful, there will be a point when you must act. Don't become a victim to "analysis paralysis." In most cases, moving forward with an effortful plan that's half-baked is better than not taking action at all.

Keep in mind this applies to instances that require quick decision making, not everyday decisions when you have ample time to develop a well-thought-out plan. During a true crisis when actions need to be taken, the worst thing you can do is to fight the urge to act. You see this most often in organizations that have several levels of hierarchy, where leaders are afraid to make a decision and would rather defer to someone else.

Learning

Find ways to learn from all your experiences. I'm a lifelong learner. Whether it's structured academic programs, online courses, conversations with loved ones, or mistakes at work, there's something to be learned from every experience. As a leader, you should be identifying learning opportunities daily.

> **There's something to be learned every day, and the minute you stop learning, you become obsolete.**

I'm not suggesting you need to rigorously study everything around you. Look at your leadership opportunities almost as real-life experiments. Please understand, I'm not advocating performing experiments in your role. What I mean is that as leaders, we get to see the best and worst of our employees and ourselves, and we get to find catered ways to respond to each. We're faced with the need to balance personal emotions while remaining even keeled and helping our employees in the work environment.

Pivoting

We get to adapt our experience and expertise to solve new problems. Through it all we have an opportunity to experiment with and adapt our skills to meet others where they are and not apply a one-size-fits-all approach.

Not everything you come up with will be a grand slam, so you must learn how to pivot. Always remain nimble enough to adjust or make modifications when things aren't going according to plan. You can think of it as course-correcting a ship to find a more efficient route or to circumvent danger.

Your work as a leader is never done, and the moment you hit cruise control is the moment all heck breaks loose.

I've witnessed compounded mistakes within an organization because leaders were afraid to admit defeat and instead wasted energy and resources pursuing a dead end, attempting to protect their egos. Don't be afraid to make changes and pivot if an unforeseen issue arises. Don't compound mistakes when you have time to pivot strategy in a way that will achieve desired results. Your employees will recognize your actions and emulate them when faced with similar circumstances.

Implementing

Acting, learning, and pivoting all contribute to putting the rubber to the road — implementing. Implementing is the time to put your money where your mouth is. Thinking, planning, and strategizing all have their place in long-term strategic planning, but there comes a time when you just need to put something in place and let the chips fall where they may.

Implementation can be hard for some people because of the fear of failure. The great thing is, I already let you know that as a leader you'll make mistakes, so the pressure's off. I wish it were that easy. It can be difficult taking the plunge sometimes by putting a decision in place because it makes us vulnerable. However, remember that vulnerability is the TAPE that keeps an organization together. If your team witnesses your ability to implement when the time is right, they're likely to do the same. Knowing when to stop talking and start doing can lead to innovations that wouldn't occur otherwise.

Never Giving Up

While it can be a personal mantra, I view never giving up as a powerful action. Easy to understand, never giving up simply means don't quit. Oftentimes everyone is given three choices when the going gets tough. You either do nothing, keep going, or you quit, all of which are "actions." If you don't think doing nothing or quitting is an action, you need to do some research, because it takes a lot of energy to not do something or to quit.

The decision to never give up and keep going is the only action that demonstrates persistence and perseverance. Different from pivoting, when you should course correct to improve results, never giving up means persisting and persevering when it's the right thing to do, even if the world around you is telling you otherwise.

As a leader you'll be put in situations in which giving up is easier than staying the course. However, just because something is easy doesn't mean it's right. The situation could be developing an employee when others are telling you to fire them, or the situation could be pushing for diverse hiring panels to encourage a diverse pipeline of qualified applicants for a job when others are satisfied with status quo.

The bottom line is: don't give up when you know your decision is right given the circumstances you face. The worst thing that could happen is you're wrong and make a mistake, but we've covered that.

Evaluating

Evaluate goes hand in hand with **Common Pitfall #2: Not Learning from Your Mistakes**. The difference with evaluate is that it's done not just when things go wrong but more importantly when things are going right. If your role involves creating new projects, launching initiatives, developing services, or building teams, there will be no shortage of things to evaluate.

Evaluate means to assess results. You shouldn't be so obsessed with assessing results that you ignore the big picture, but you should regularly evaluate key aspects and programs. Consider how to evaluate the impact to core business functions and potentially the impact on employee well-being. Only through the appropriate evaluation of core business functions will you be able to identify areas for improvement.

Understanding different leadership styles you might identify with is the first step to developing your authenticity. Based on your style, certain behaviors can and will make or break your relationships with your employees. Further emphasizing the need for you to relate with one or several styles, emerging trends in leadership and the workplace could require you to reconsider your approach. Regardless of the style you finally land on, you'll likely encounter one or more leadership pitfalls along the way. Encountering a pitfall does not mean automatic failure if you put tactics in place that allow you to ascend to ALPINE heights.

Key Takeaways

1	All leaders make mistakes, without exception. Own your mistakes and move on.
2	You can learn a lot from mistakes, so make it part of your standard practice. You don't want to keep making the same mistakes.
3	When things get rough, try to keep a level head to tell the difference between a crisis and a bad day. Your team will respond better in an actual crisis, and taking time to collect yourself could reduce the magnitude of a mistake if it's made during a crisis.
4	Recognize the signs of imposter syndrome in yourself and your team. It can happen to anyone, and it's a self-defeating thought process that doesn't give bearing to the hard work and effort a person puts in to get where they are. Imposter syndrome hurts the person it affects. Left unaddressed, it can start to hurt their work, too.
5	When facing challenges or common leadership pitfalls, remember the **ALPINE** tactics: acting, learning, pivoting, implementing, never giving up, and evaluating.

Be Realistic:
Goal Setting
& Development

We've all heard the optimistic saying that goes something like, "You can be anything you want to be as long as you put your mind to it." I hope I don't burst anyone's bubble, but that isn't true at all — at least in my lived experience. I've always wanted to be in the military, but I have asthma. No matter how hard I put my mind to it, I will always have asthma, and as a result I'm automatically disqualified from the military. Unfortunately, that's my reality, and I had to come to terms with it.

However, the sooner I came to terms with it, the better prepared I was to explore alternatives. I think that longing for the military is what drew me to law enforcement. Once I set my goal of getting into law enforcement, I was able to work on developing the necessary skills the profession requires. I knew there were minimum education requirements to apply, and there would be an acceptable standard of physical conditioning to be effective at the job. I also knew I could start getting relevant experience by seeking employment in a related field like security.

For the next two and a half years after setting the goal of becoming a police officer, I took administration of justice courses and started working in security guarding. It took me two different attempts but, once I was qualified to apply, I was hired by the San Jose Police Department. The day I pinned my official badge on was the first day of the rest of my life. While I would've loved to have served in the military, law enforcement was a rewarding career that helped cast the mold of the leader I am today.

To be a successful corporate leader, you need to be realistic with your abilities and those of your team members. Realism comes not just from recognizing a person's limitations but also in identifying opportunities. I think the latter often goes unrecognized. Like the trends I discussed in **Chapter 7: Workplace Emerging Trends** where companies need to start to shift their focus to improving inclusivity and well-being, companies also need to start focusing on opportunities for employees. That's the heart of being realistic.

Companies need to prioritize employee development — including leadership development — identify opportunities for growth, and use goal-setting not only to measure performance but also to push employees toward career progression.

There's often an idea that investing in employee development and career progression is a zero-sum game. Meaning that for employees to gain something, the company needs to lose something. I've seen it time and time again. When considering third-party training programs or paying for an employee to take a training course, the question of relevance always comes up.

As if it's Goldilocks sampling porridge, companies want a balance that's just right. They don't want employees to attend training that's too far outside their scope, advancing their skills, else they may seek gainful employment elsewhere. They also don't want employees to attend training that's completely unrelated, for the same reason.

Let's be realistic, the era of employees staying with a company right out of college into their golden years is long gone. Employees will come and go. The question then becomes: wouldn't you want employees to feel supported, leverage new skills, and develop into better versions of themselves while they're still with you?

If you can leverage the skill of your employees while they're learning and developing, as well as identify new opportunities for them in your organization at the same time, you have a better chance of employee retention. This can all be fostered within the organization through professional development and goal setting.

Chapter 9: Goal Setting

With the prolific use of GPS apps that offer turn-by-turn directions such as Apple Maps, Google Maps, or Waze, I wonder how I ever found anything before. I hail from the era that used foldable paper maps, and to be honest, a part of me misses those days.

I recall working patrol, when I was working for the San Jose Police Department, having about twenty pages of laminated and highly detailed "beat maps." The beat maps outlined the area of responsibility for a specific portion of the city, or a "beat."

Before GPS was as reliable as it is nowadays, I spent my time plotting out locations in my beat and learning shortcuts through the city. I would come up with acronyms to identify the major connecting streets that worked like arteries in my beat. The reason for all the effort was that when a crisis or emergency was happening, I didn't have time to waste figuring out directions by pulling out a large beat map. I had to know the path to take to get me to my destination like it was second nature. Any delay could mean loss of life.

While not as dire, goal setting in a corporate environment isn't much different. As a successful corporate leader, you need to make sure your team always knows the purpose, destination, and goal of the company and department. Then, foster an environment that permeates alignment with your goals, in all actions, so your team will invest their actions to achieve the identified goals.

Your goals are a lighthouse for your team. When situations become murky, or targets start to become unclear, your team knows they can align themselves with the lighthouse to get back on track and avoid veering off course.

Achieving Alignment

Your team's goals can take on a few different forms as short-, mid-, and long-term goals, but regardless of the form, goals are the raison d'être. An often-used term, raison d'être is French for "reason for being." Your employees need to embrace your goals in the form of mission, vision, and objectives so passionately that everything they do aligns to your goals as if it were part of their nature. (Not that your team's reason for existence is to serve your company.) This may sound overly ambitious to some, but I believe it's essential for a successful corporate leader to understand.

Goal setting has another valuable component aside from the corporate focus, and that's when it comes to personal goal setting. In parallel with employees aligning their efforts to meet company needs, a leader can ensure an employee's needs are being met along the way. I have a sincere belief that no one intentionally wants to be a bad employee. The problem is that employees become disenfranchised for a variety of reasons throughout their career.

You need to use the same goal-setting techniques used for setting company and department goals to help employees set professional development and career goals. When done properly, employees will remain invigorated in their roles, which leads to improved contributions to the organization.

While this isn't accomplished overnight and isn't a straightforward process, the fantastic news is that if you can foster a company that constantly creates employee goals aligned with organizational goals, it'll become part of the culture. Culture eats strategy for breakfast. A culture that constantly promotes employee development in line with corporate goals will reinforce company strategy to the point that it's an immutable force.

Company and Department Goals

There are three types of organizational goals: vision, mission, and objectives — **VMO**. While the three sound similar and are often used interchangeably, there are nuances. In this case, their respective priorities and definitions are:

Vision (What?)	Long-term focused
Mission (How?)	Mid-term focused
Objectives (Now!)	Short-term focused

Vision

Vision is the main priority. Vision ends up being the north star for the organization. It creates the kindling that sparks passion for an employee's purpose. Mission and objectives help support a company's vision by creating the foundation for action that can move mountains.

Let's look at Google's vision: "to provide access to the world's information in one click." This is a clearcut vision — a long-term goal, focused on the future. This creates the "what" for the company. You'll often notice that clearly stated visions are lofty. There are no specific timelines or hard and fast numbers. Visions are set to inspire others to aspire for greatness.

Google uses the words "world's information." Those two simple words imply "all" of the world's information. Not to mention having all that information available "in one click." Those are tremendous goals, but it helps to keep the company focused on the future. This will help the company maintain focus on the products it creates, the tools it refines, and even the companies it chooses to partner with.

From a company perspective, Google's vision is great, but what if you're a successful corporate leader in a supporting department? Let's say you work in facilities management and want to create a vision for your department that aligns with the company vision. Your vision could be something like, "Create environments that inspire." Another lofty vision, but for a facilities management department it overlaps nicely with the company vision and is specific, and applicable, within the department. Regardless of your seniority, having a vision statement can be a valuable tool.

Mission

Google's mission is "to organize the world's information and make it universally accessible and useful." This mission is clearly defined and easy to digest. While it can be seen as more mid-term focused, it's still lofty.

The mission starts to define the "how" — how they expect to achieve the company's vision. The "how" is the action. A lofty vision without action is daydreaming. For Google, the mission of "organizing the world's information and making it universally accessible" is the action necessary to accomplish the vision, "to provide access to the world's information in one click." The vision and mission provide the company's foundation for who they are.

Continuing with our facilities department example, if the vision is to, "Create environments that inspire," then a supporting mission could be, "Deliver efficient facilities services that develop accessible and welcoming workplaces."

Just like the vision, the mission for the facilities department is relevant to the type of work they'll do while supporting the company vision and mission. When you have clear vision and mission statements, developing clear objectives will be easier.

Objectives

Objectives can have any number of names such as key results, targets, or goals. Regardless of what name you pre-scribe to objectives, an objective includes the short-term actions and steps required to accomplish a task. Objectives can be project-based assignments, quarterly targets, or annual results. While objectives dictate what work gets done daily, they should always be aligned to the company vision and mission.

The most effective way for a leader to ensure that is the case is to create department-specific visions and missions, like our facilities example above. A facilities department will contribute to the company vision and mission differently than a human resources department.

Creating a VMO for Your Team

Regardless of whether you're creating something from scratch or refining what you already have in place, these five considerations when developing your own VMO will help you create goals in a **BLINC** of an eye that are:

BROAD
LINKED
INCLUSIVE
NIMBLE
CONSIDERATE

Broad

Broad VMOs aren't so precise that goals become a to-do list. To-do lists help keep track of what needs to get done. However, they're short, specific, and rarely does anyone review their to-do lists after they're done. Keeping goals for VMOs broad helps prevent the mindset of "one and done." It helps to set goals just enough out of reach that there's always something else to be done. It's this type of action and mindset that sparks innovation.

Linked

It's especially important when creating a department vision and mission to ensure that they're linked to the broader company. It serves no purpose to create opposing goals that don't link or align with the company. This is worse than having no goals at all because your lighthouse is sending your department in the wrong direction.

Inclusive

The way to avoid this is by being inclusive in the process of creating your goals. By including employees and essential stakeholders in the process of developing VMOs, you'll not only be more likely to ensure linked goals, but more importantly you'll also get employee buy-in.

Like building a deck for your home, training for a marathon, or even starting a business, you were more likely fully committed, even when things got tough, because it was something you chose to do. If a neighbor asked for your help on a household project, you might lend a hand. But if you noticed your neighbor was starting to watch more than work or disappear completely, you wouldn't hang around for very long. The same can be said about creating VMOs. Being inclusive and allowing employees to help set the goals will help them contribute to the creation of their raison d'être. It'll also help your employees understand that you're an equitable decision maker, which can go a long way.

Nimble

When done right, you shouldn't change your vision and mission very often. However, you should create objectives that allow you to be nimble. While avoiding a "to-do list" mentality, you also need to make sure the language allows you to move quickly and resourcefully. No one knows what the future holds. Today's solutions are tomorrow's problems. Your goals must be nimble enough to quickly pivot when faced with tomorrow's problems, otherwise where you should have innovation, you'll have implosion.

Considerate

Lastly, VMOs should be considerate of the population they're meant to serve. If your goals are self-serving, it'll be very hard to get your employees or stakeholders to buy into your purpose.

Take Google for example. While they have a dominant advertising presence, I don't think anyone would buy into their company if their vision was, "To provide access to the world's information [so we can generate millions of dollars] in one click." While that might be Google's business model, that's not why the employees do their work. Their vision is considerate of the population they want to serve, in this case "the world."

Setting VMOs for an organization is essential for a successful corporate leader. VMOs serve as a lighthouse and raison d'être for employees and contribute to their investment in the organization. While some may see it as a laborious task, developing and setting appropriate VMOs can be done in the BLINC of an eye.

Key Takeaways

1	Goals are a lighthouse for your team. When situations become murky or targets start to become unclear, your team knows they can align themselves with the lighthouse to get back on track and avoid veering off course.
2	**VMO**: Vision is a long-term goal, focused on the future. Mission starts to define how the company expects to achieve this vision in the mid-term. Objectives (key results, targets, or goals) are the short-term actions and steps required to accomplish something, and they should always be aligned to the company vision and mission.
3	A successful corporate leader needs to use the same goal-setting techniques used for setting organizational and company goals to help employees set professional development and career goals. This helps employees feel supported, leverage their skills, and remain engaged with the organization, which can help with employee retention.

Chapter 10: Providing Leadership with Realism

Managing with Concern and Authenticity help provide a working foundation to lead with Realism. As a successful corporate leader, you need to understand (and realize) that not everything you do will be a home run, and not every employee you manage will respond with record levels of commitment no matter how great the **VMO**.

While the administrative execution of VMOs is a necessity, you must be able to follow up with effective leadership skills to help others navigate the perilous journey that is career progression. In doing so, you must be realistic about what your employees can expect of you and you of them. Leadership is a **SURE** thing, and even if your investment in others doesn't immediately pay off, you can rest assured that as a successful corporate leader you'll have done everything in your power to selflessly help others in their journey.

The tips I provide in this chapter will assist you with demonstrating realism. Improve your leadership skills to be real with your employees and **BEAM DOOD**:

BE PRESENT
EXERCISE MINDFULNESS
ACKNOWLEDGE CAREER STAGNATION
MANAGE BY WALKING AROUND

DOOR OPEN,
OPEN
OPEN
DOOR

Be Present

Being present is undervalued. This one is so simple that it's easily overlooked, but it can be a powerful skill. Being present means being actively engaged with your employees during meetings and conversations and keeping your mind actively engaged without distraction.

This translates into refraining from checking a text message, reading email, answering a phone call, or planning for your next meeting while you are engaged with others. Most importantly, it means practicing active listening, an essential communication skill. (Learn about active listening in depth in **Chapter 15: Communication Methods**.)

For me, this is exactly why I acknowledge my limits and ask my team to keep meetings requiring concentrated cognitive investment in the morning. I want to make sure I can be fully present when my team is meeting with me. I think we can all identify multiple times in our lives, even within the past day, where either a manager, colleague, friend, or significant other was not "present" for us. It's an awful feeling to think your leader is going through the motions during a 1:1 meeting or presentation that you worked hard to complete.

Being present is an invaluable skill, and sometimes it takes some effort to do it right, but once you master it, you'll find you've taken your leadership skills to the next level. We can all appreciate feeling like we've been heard because others are mentally present when we're speaking. For employees, having a leader who's present will help instill trust and contribute to their psychological safety and well-being.

Exercise Mindfulness

Mindfulness is something that's been gaining attention in the business environment for some time. Admittedly, when I studied mindfulness for my master's degree, I was skeptical. However, for the past two years, I've actively practiced mindfulness, and it's done wonders for maintaining mental clarity.

Mindfulness can take on many forms. Experiment with what works best for you. Once perfected, I highly encourage you to share the following four mindfulness activities with your employees.

Mindfulness can be as valuable as **JEMS**, by:

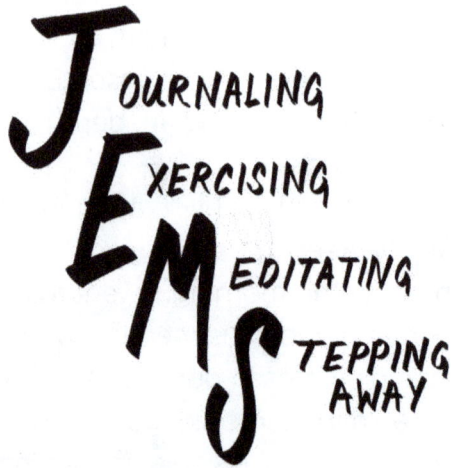

JOURNALING
EXERCISING
MEDITATING
STEPPING AWAY

Journaling

It took me some time to appreciate the value of journaling, but now I've enjoyed that skill for more than three years. I call it a skill because it takes effort to journal well. Some people think of journaling and immediately think of a diary, but it's much more than that. Journaling is not a to-do list and not an account of daily activities, that's a diary. The basics of journaling is setting intentional time aside regularly to write out your thoughts, feelings, and insights in a free-flowing manner.

I journal first thing in the morning about four to five days per week. It's ritualistic in that I wake up early in the morning, grab my morning beverage, and walk up to my writing desk. I don't journal at my work desk because I don't want to be distracted with the urge to open my work computer.

Once I'm at my writing desk, I open my refillable leather journal and sniff the inside of the leather. I absolutely love the smell of leather and can't help myself. Smelling my journal also stimulates my olfactory senses, setting the stage for writing.

Then I take out my mechanical pencil — I only journal in pencil because I need to feel the interaction of graphite on the page — and open the journal to the next blank page. I then write anything and everything on my mind for fifteen to twenty minutes. I've written about fears, aspirations, desires, worries, happiness, and philosophies, and I've never gone back to read what I've previously written.

The point of journaling is not to maintain a running log of activity. For me it's a space for me to write out random thoughts. I've found that doing so removes inhibiting thoughts that could affect me in the workplace. We all have thoughts running through our mind that never make it anywhere. Some of these thoughts are productive and others are counterproductive and get bottled-up.

Journaling is a way to "exercise" your mind, releasing the bottled-up pressure. Journaling has removed some serious mental barriers and has improved my leadership ability.

Exercising

As you learn to exercise your brain through journaling, you must also learn how to exercise your body. We all start to feel the pressure of stress from life and leadership. Whether it's family, friends, work, or finances, there's no shortage of sources producing anxiety and stress. You need to find a way to expend all that built-up stress on a regular basis.

Let's be clear. I'm not talking about getting into shape or maintaining physical fitness. While both are important, you only need to find exercise appropriate for your lifestyle. This can take the form of a sport, like golf or basketball, high-intensity interval training, riding a bike, or something as simple as walking.

Whatever you choose, it should be something that gets your heart pumping a little, causes you to breathe a bit faster, and gets the blood flowing to all your extremities. Aside from all the medical benefits associated with exercise, for you as a leader it'll help to relieve some of the stress accrued throughout the day.

Meditating

Some of you may cringe at the thought of meditating, but like exercise, this too can take many forms. I define meditation as the intentional act of achieving a heightened state of awareness and focused attention. I won't go into all the ways you can mediate; you can research that on your own. Instead, let's focus on the definition I laid out.

I meditate on the days I journal. After having expelled my pent-up thoughts, I sit in my writing chair and practice some deep breathing. I then bring attention to my entire body, allowing myself to relax. After a couple of minutes, I choose to do some Bible study to keep my attention on something other than myself. I intentionally focus on the words I'm reading, allowing my mind to wander and drift while it processes the message on the page. If my thoughts start to wander on the day's events, I stop reading, refocus my breath, and bring myself back into awareness of my body. I continue this for a total of fifteen minutes.

Your method and medium will vary depending on the tools that are meaningful to you, but the act of meditating teaches me to focus my attention, control my thoughts, and practice intentional breathing. These essential skills will help you maintain awareness of your thoughts and surroundings as you navigate your own environment.

Stepping Away

Lastly, stepping away is a straightforward concept I've introduced as a method of prioritizing your needs. However, it's worth bringing up as an active skill that doesn't just require stepping away for a vacation. Stepping away is knowing when you literally need to remove yourself from your surroundings.

How many times have you been in an argument with a significant other, family member, or friend to the point where both people were hot under the collar? Of those previous arguments, how many times did something slip past your lips that you wish you could immediately take back?

We all know that once something slips past your lips there's no rewind or delete button. That's when stepping away comes into effect. As a leader, if you allow your emotions to get the best of you and verbally say or type something you shouldn't, then there could be endless repercussions. People management is a SURE thing, and as a result not everything will be rosy every day. There have been many times I've drafted an email in a state of elevated emotional response and was wise enough to walk away to let things simmer down. More often than not, I would return to the email, delete what was written, and compose a new, more appropriate email before pressing send.

Take advantage of the beauty in JEMS to organize your thoughts and reconsider your response in a reduced and relaxed mental state. Sometimes I'll ruminate on a response for a full day to exercise mindfulness, and every time I'm better off for it.

Acknowledge Career Stagnation

You may have had a double take at this listed leadership skill for being realistic, but it isn't wrong. With very few exceptions, the same role for the same person in the same company for years on end doesn't inspire employee commitment. Closely related to the well-being trend in **Chapter 9: Goal Setting**, gone are the days when employees would be satisfied with spending their entire career at the same job from an entry-level position into their golden years.

One of the primary reasons for the loss of employee motivation and decreased performance is career stagnation. This can occur for many reasons, but there are three primary ones that require acknowledgment: a lack of continued professional development, absent career progression, and a mix of the two.

The lack of continued professional development is a responsibility of the employee, but it requires a successful corporate leader to identify with their employees. I've experienced many conversations with employees who want to do more or desire a promotion, but when confronted, they admit they haven't done anything to improve their skill set to prepare them for the next role.

Worse yet, I've held performance conversations where employees readily admit they don't like their job and deeply desire another role but don't put forth the effort to gain the skills they need to cross over into something different.

There is where I've recognized the growing trend toward accountability. You need to help your employees recognize they have just as much responsibility as, if not more than, you as their leader to accomplish their career goals.

I always tell my employees, "You are your biggest advocate for your career. If you don't relentlessly pursue new opportunities and advocate for yourself, no one else will do it for you." Once you can get your employees to take accountability for their career, you can make efforts like stretching them into other opportunities or connecting them with a mentor to enlighten them to the skills necessary for a certain role.

When employees are invested in their own growth and working with you, you can help them acknowledge areas they may immediately be able to start developing. It could be taking on additional responsibilities like budget management, contract creation, or even leading a project meeting.

I once had an employee who was terrified of budgeting but admitted learning the skill would help him with a promotion. With his agreement, he assisted me with creating the department annual forecast. The first time he helped me, I was hand-holding throughout the entire process beginning to end. The following year, I hardly had to lift a finger because his skill, confidence, and capability grew to manage the process independently. The employee ended up with a promotion.

Unfortunately, there are organizations and positions where career progression is completely absent. You tend to see this in tech companies in which entry-level niche roles have a ceiling that's clearly identified, and career progression isn't possible.

These types of roles are very challenging. For leaders, there's an unofficial countdown timer from when employees start off motivated and excited because they're happy to be with the company to the time that excitement fades and they're restless for something new. For employees, if a leader isn't transparent about existing limits to career growth, they're likely to harbor resentment once it's discovered, and performance could quickly deteriorate. The best thing you can do in these instances is quickly identify what your employees desire and take a proactive approach to helping them find other opportunities they can strive to gain over time.

By identifying opportunities and guiding employees toward obtaining the necessary skills to gain opportune roles, a successful corporate leader can extend the countdown timer. Advocating for an employee through allyship can take the form of praising in public or sending a special department recognition leading to increased attention from other leaders and potential new managers.

Many companies have some tool in the way of an employee award, company newsletter, or department meeting where an employee's positive contributions can take center stage. Appropriately casting light on an employee's contributions can gain the attention of a leader with an open role. Managers are more likely to hire an employee they've heard about, especially if that employee is excelling in their role and has developed the necessary skills to be considered.

The third contributor to career stagnation, a combination of the previous two occurrences, is the worst yet. Sometimes employees are in a role that has limited potential, and they don't have the motivation to develop the skills necessary to do something else. This is a recipe for disaster. A successful corporate leader needs to quickly acknowledge these types of situations and monitor them closely.

It doesn't always mean the situation will end badly, but the likelihood of someone calling off regularly or doing a no-call, no-show is high. The best thing you can do is show **CARE** regardless of how long an employee might be in the role.

The most useful tool, discussed in the next section, is to express empathy for these employees. They'll be shoved between a rock and a hard place knowing they don't have a career path and are with no desire to grow into something else. Guide, coach, and mentor those in this type of "dead-end role," so that when they do walk away, by choice or force, they leave feeling you invested in them.

Manage by Walking Around

Manage by walking around (MBWA) is a widely accepted concept in business. **MBWA** simply means engaging with employees while purposefully meandering through the office environment. This is simple enough to understand, but there are a couple of nuances.

Most important is that MBWA should not be done in a way that silently indicates you are "checking up" on employees. If you were to MBWA at the same time every day, let's say right before "quitting time," employees would see the action as negative rather than something positive. Instead, you need to vary how often and what time you MBWA.

It's also important you don't have a hidden agenda. The intent isn't to sneak up on others or try to conduct an "investigation" of the staff. Instead, you should allow encounters to happen organically and allow your team to take the conversation where they'd like to. The whole purpose of MBWA is allowing employees to feel like their leader is accessible, approachable, and open-minded.

Some office settings have become a hybrid format of in-person and work-from-home, which provides an interesting twist to this skill, but I still believe there's a way to accomplish MBWA successfully.

While not as organic, nothing precludes a leader from scheduling an impromptu fifteen-minute chat with their direct and indirect employees during the week. This can be tricky because you don't want to schedule it too far in advance or last minute on the same day. That could cause an employee to think something's wrong.

However, if you were to send out a few invites every Monday for later in the week, your team would quickly adapt and be less wary about what the meeting's about. After a while, employees would become desensitized to the calendar invite, grow to appreciate it, and learn to utilize the time to openly communicate. MBWA goes a long way for a successful corporate leader when they're also providing their full attention to their employees.

Door Open, Open Door

Door open, open door (**DOOD**) policy (I just couldn't help myself with the DOOD acronym) speaks to being accessible to your employees. Nearly every company embraces an open door (OD) policy in which employees are encouraged to bring concerns, suggestions, and complaints to their respective managers without fear of repercussions.

Something I picked up from a previous manager, a door open (DO) policy literally means leaving your office door open, inviting your team to approach you. Understand there will be times when you need to have your door closed for meetings, but that doesn't mean it's all the time.

So, you may be wondering what the difference between the two, DO vs. OD is. If your team felt comfortable and psychologically safe enough to approach you with a concern, but you were always inaccessible because your office door was closed, would you really have an open door policy?

What good is an open door policy if no one felt like you were accessible? I believe you can't have one without the other. Like MBWA, as a leader you need to be accessible, approachable, and open-minded, and the only way to do that is with a DO policy.

This skill also conflicts with a hybrid environment of in-person and work-from-home employees, but I offer a work around. Separate from scheduling time with your team through MBWA, you could send out fifteen-minute time slots to your entire organization on a first-come, first-serve basis each week for sign-ups.

Similarly, create open meeting slots on your calendar and use your company chat or meeting software to create "pop-ins." You can create a video meeting space in a work chat or calendar and send out a link to the meeting during your dedicated time slots for employees to pop in.

Whichever method you use, make sure you're engaged in an activity that's not too mentally taxing and can be interrupted. You don't want to be heavily engaged in something only to appear distracted when an employee does pop in expecting to have your full attention.

Accessibility cannot be over emphasized. As a leader you'll be constantly investing in your employees, and they're your best resource for understanding the health of the entire organization. If you don't create a culture of accessibility, your culture will eat your strategy for breakfast.

Key Takeaways

1	Improve your leadership skills to be real with your employees and **BEAM DOOD** by being present, exercising mindfulness, acknowledging career stagnation, managing by walking around, and maintaining a door open, open door policy.
2	Know that mindfulness can be as valuable as **JEMS** by journaling, exercising, meditating, and stepping away.
3	Encourage employees to take control of their professional development. Especially if an employee is in a role with a clear ceiling, proactively help them identify skills they can develop and opportunities they could pursue.
4	Career stagnation can occur for a variety of reasons and requires a leader to partner with their employees to develop essential skills that'll advance them in a new opportunity.

Chapter 11: Performance Development

We have now arrived at what I believe to be the heart of being a successful corporate leader — performance development. I define performance development as the constant investment in others to help grow their sense of self to meet the expectations of a job, meet life's challenges, or fulfill a purpose. Performance development is where realism takes shape. Consisting of two major buckets, performance development includes performance enablement and performance management.

I never understood the value of performance development until I was a manager for Meta. Ironically, it wasn't even that I had some epiphany. It took Mary Jane talking some sense into me to understand what performance development really was. I mentioned this in **Chapter 8: Common Pitfalls to Avoid**, but I was suffering from a brutal case of imposter syndrome at Meta when Mary Jane pulled me into a meeting. I'd been second guessing actions on a project and hadn't been assertive enough as the project lead to the point where the project was starting to fall behind schedule.

Mary Jane was blunt and to the point without any sugar coating. She sat me down and didn't even ask what was going on with me. She simply stated, "You need to get out of your own head. I hired you for a reason, and your skill is what this project needs. Now do what you need to do to shake off whatever is going on and be the manager I know you are."

That was all it took; she was 100 percent right. I was allowing myself to be sucked into worry and doubt. I wasn't accepting that I was an expert, and I was the project lead for a reason. That was when the light bulb turned on for me. Leading up to that point, Mary Jane was using "kid gloves," gently nudging me with hopes it would be enough to wake me up. Once she realized I wasn't responding to the gentle approach, she took the more hardline approach to get through to me, and that was what I needed.

As a leader your responsibility will be to know when to be gentle or to nosedive into your employee's head to get their performance to improve. Had I not responded by improving my performance, Mary Jane wouldn't have hesitated to take a more assertive approach to performance improvement.

Breakdown of Performance Enablement and Performance Management

When it comes to the workplace, you have a variety of tools at your disposal that contribute to the performance development of their employees. Two of the tools that often get misconstrued, but are very relevant, are performance enablement and performance management.

Performance enablement is leader-focused, based on the direct and indirect actions that you take to help develop others. Performance management is employee-focused and involves developing a person's skill to meet the current demands of a role and building resilience.

The people management and leadership industry rely too much on internal performance improvement policies, a nested element within performance management, that are only called upon when something's going wrong. There needs to be a shift in thought where performance management is an always-on practice, and hard and fast performance improvement is a last resort.

Let me explain this with an example from my time in law enforcement. As part of the police academy, there's one domain that serves as a great equalizer for those who want to become full-time police officers.

Most people would assume that firearms handling is the greatest of equalizers, after all you're learning how to operate a lethal weapon, and a failure within the public has far more ramifications than a failure in the academy. Because of the historical failure rate in police academies, students are given hours and hours of opportunity to remedy failure to become proficient at handling a deadly weapon before they can graduate.

Because of the many retraining opportunities provided for firearms, I posit that the greatest of equalizers is vehicle handling. In my academy, this was referred to as the Emergency Vehicle Operations Course (EVOC). You had a limited amount of time behind the wheel because the courses were complex, and the equipment was specialized. Not only was the behind-the-wheel training intense, but so was the amount of classroom hours spent learning vehicle dynamics and driver psychology.

The entire forty-hour course ended with the dreaded ten-minute-long pursuit. As part of the final test there was literally a "cone city" with a thousand cones simulating streets, alleys, and long bends. The test started off with you "patrolling" your cone city. Then you were informed over the radio of a vehicle associated with a felony crime against persons. Low and behold you would spot the vehicle, driven by one of the instructors, and then you were off to the races.

You had to successfully broadcast radio transmissions as you were in pursuit while not allowing the instructor vehicle to get neither too far ahead nor too close. For ten minutes you were navigating high-speed areas, entering sharp turns, tight "L" shape alleys, and slalom type street designs, all while also updating your radio at appropriate times.

Some of you who haven't been through this type of training might be wondering, so what's the big deal? You may be thinking how cool it is to drive fast and furious for ten minutes and play chase. Those of you who have been through this may be recalling your own driving experience and the high blood pressure and body sweats associated with your academy days.

Here's the kicker, for those who don't already know what determines a pass or fail, not only do you have to do everything I mentioned — operating a radio, staying an "appropriate" distance from the instructor vehicle, and following the exact path with no shortcuts — but you also must do so without so much as touching one of the thousand cones on the ground.

That's right. If you so much as nick the base of the cone, let alone flat out hit one, you fail. No returning to "Go", no mulligans, no take backsies. If you hit a cone, your academy career is potentially over. Most academies allow a second try, but fail again, and you're out.

To some, especially those who went through this gauntlet and failed to emerge triumphant, this can seem extreme. However, we were often reminded that you'll spend thousands of hours driving your patrol car, a lot more than you'll ever fire your gun in the field, and a "cone" in an academy course represents a person in real life. There just isn't any room for error, and yet you get a lot less time to practice your driving skills than you do shooting your gun on the firing range. Hence, the EVOC course is the greatest of equalizers.

So, what does this have to do with performance development? While I certainly hope your leadership decisions won't result in a constant balance of life-and-death scenarios, there's certainly a need to operate with as little error as possible.

You can think of the mean streets of "cone city" as workplace obstacles and unknowns, and the instructor vehicle as the VMOs being chased. The right vehicle, properly equipped for the pursuit, can be thought of as performance enablement, and the instructor giving specific training and guidance to the driver is performance management. Together, the vehicle and driver/instructor combo make up performance development.

Like operating a high-speed emergency vehicle, performance development is a constant process balancing management and enablement. I view performance management as employee-centric, or activity based. In my driving example, performance management is equivalent to an instructor teaching the student what to do and them doing it.

For example, an instructor may provide an understanding of how spring loading can lead to a loss of traction or how to correct for understeer/oversteer. The instructor can teach the philosophy of what to do and why, but the student is the one who needs to perform the action in a specific situation.

The instructor manages the performance of the student and the actions they take. Performance management in the workplace requires a manager focusing on how to guide employees' actions, thoughts, and doubts, as well as helping them understand how to navigate through difficulty, away from potential tragedy, and toward success.

The instructor represents the leader, and the driver is the employee expected to execute. However, a successful corporate leader must also provide the right vehicle, in the form of performance enablement, to get the job done. But what happens if the driver fails the driving test? Tradition has taught us to put all the blame on the driver, but we fail to look at the instructor.

Taking away the analogies, the people management and leadership industry has taught us to put all blame on employees when things go wrong and not the manager. Performance enablement on the part of a successful corporate leader moves the needle, allowing for managerial accountability when employees fail.

Leadership Fatigue

Remember that operating as a successful corporate leader, investing time to develop others, is a **SURE** thing. It's selfless, unending, rewarding, and exhausting. Over time it'll take its toll on you because true performance development is a constant, active process. You need to make sure you're taking full advantage of **JEMS** to maximize your mindfulness.

Some of you could be wondering why I bring up the idea of leadership fatigue as a theme so frequently. It's because I don't think it's given enough attention in any industry. Leaders are only human and as such are fallible, emotional, and sometimes easily influenced. Learning how to balance external influences so that you, as a leader, are always able to maintain objectivity and put everyone's needs before your own is something that won't necessarily be natural. Since it's unnatural, it'll take intentional effort and require constant attention to do correctly. Because of the constant investment in others, you'll start to lose focus on yourself.

Your needs are just as important as those of your employees. After all, I really hope that what you're learning from *Lead with CARE* is shared knowledge with a leader you report to, and you're feeling some support by employing the skills learned here. Performance development will be the most demanding aspect of your role as a leader, and you need to be real with yourself and leverage JEMS, so you'll be prepared to balance the demands placed on you.

Environmental and External Factors

Demands will come in all sorts of shapes and sizes. A leader and their employees will be subject to influence by an ever-changing internal corporate environment and an even more unpredictable external environment, both of which could potentially derail all the positive performance development a leader will put into place.

Using an example, one of my previous employees, Gwen, had been struggling at work. I'd developed work goals, a regular 1:1 meeting, and guided Gwen to work on projects that focused on her strengths. Over three months Gwen's performance started to improve, and she was trending toward positive performance. Then we went through a reorganization and my responsibilities changed, so Gwen became an indirect employee reporting to a new manager.

Gwen felt defeated, and her performance reverted to needing improvement. Ultimately, the responsibility to perform rested with Gwen, but I still felt responsible for her development. It took another three months before she was able to pick herself up and meet the expectations of the job, but it was an example of not being able to control all aspects of the internal corporate environment. My performance development efforts were stalled because of something out of my control. Fortunately, Gwen was able to focus and improve her performance.

Even more complicated is the effect of a person's external environment on performance. Most people can relate to the impact of the external environment which, among many other things, can take the shape of medical issues, relationship complications, health concerns of friends, other loved ones, and even pets, or worse, a combination of all the above.

The impact of the external environment on an employee's performance is a leader's worst nightmare. You have no control or visibility into what's happening in a person's life behind the scenes. There could be some negative medical prognosis they're keeping to themselves, an unsupportive home life that's draining their energy, or something that's happened to someone they care about.

Your employees' cognitive load (more on this later) can be at its max, and there's nothing you can do but offer concern, empathy, and company support. The toughest part of performance development will be balancing the needs of your employees with the needs of the company. I'm a compassionate person. While I'll support my employees and provide them with access to all available resources, there are times when I need to put the company's priorities above those of my employees. This doesn't make me a heartless dilettante but instead a successful corporate leader.

Think of it this way, some of your major corporate companies will have a plethora of resources, often referred to as employee assistance programs (EAP), to help employees through the rough times that life has to offer. But like all benefits, there's a limit.

There's also a limit to how much work, effort, and support I can offer as a successful corporate leader. However, if I successfully invested in my employees and worked to develop their skills, if it comes a time to let an employee go, then they should be leaving with more skill than when they first started. In that way, you'll always be able to benefit those you lead.

Key Takeaways

1 Performance development is a constant investment in others to help grow their sense of self to meet the expectations of a job, meet life's challenges, or fulfill a purpose.

2 Performance enablement is the direct and indirect actions that you as a leader take to help develop others.

3 Performance management involves developing a person's skill to meet the current demands of a role and building resilience.

4 Performance improvement, a nested element within performance management, is used specifically when an employee's performance is failing, and measures need to be taken to remedy said performance.

5 Performance development is an ongoing, active process, and over time this can lead to leadership fatigue.

6 You and your employees are subject to ever-changing internal corporate environments and even more unpredictable external environments, both of which can derail the positive performance development a leader puts into place.

Chapter 12: Performance Management

Performance management is the process of developing a person's skill to meet the current demands of a role and building resilience to grow beyond their current capacity.

Performance management is great when an employee is thriving, and you're nourishing their growth. However, it has a negative aspect with performance improvement.

Performance Development	
Performance Management (Employee-Centric)	**Performance Enablement (Leader-Centric)**
• 1:1 meetings • Performance conversations • Cognitive load • Motivation	• Performance review • Understanding human capital • Growth vs. fixed mindset • SMART goals

Performance improvement is mostly seen as negative because it often occurs when an employee's performance is failing, and measures need to be taken to remedy said performance. However, I hope when you're done with this chapter, you've learned performance improvement can be positive as well.

All the proposed elements are presented with the focus on the employee. As a successful corporate leader, you'll provide your employees with the tools they need to be successful and thrive. Performance management is where you'll actively work on performance improvement for employees that need assistance with meeting job expectations.

The elements of performance management include:

- **1:1 Meetings**
- **Performance Conversations**
- **Cognitive Load**
- **Motivation**

While some of the elements may overlap with one another it's important to understand the nuances between each.

1:1 Meetings

Any sort of leader is used to the concept of setting up regular meetings with their staff. However, there are some elements that are often overlooked. The most important point is 1:1 meetings need to be focused on your employee's needs. If you only use 1:1 meetings to speak one-sided about performance or discuss issues, you're not providing a safe place for employees to share their successes or communicate road blocks. Instead, you create an atmosphere where employees are discouraged to meet with their leader.

If 1:1 meetings are focused on communication with the employee and offer guidance, contributing to the employee's performance, they'll always know they have an opportunity to meet in a psychologically safe environment. Productive 1:1 meetings are a time to focus on **TRUST**:

TIMELY
RESOLVE ROADBLOCKS
UPDATES
SET EXPECTATIONS + SEEK CLARIFICATION
TRUTHFUL

Timely

All 1:1 meetings should be timely, meaning they should occur at regular and known intervals, and they should be a fixed duration. While there are several factors that determine how often you should meet with your team, and I'll leave it to you to decide, it's vital that all meetings stick to a fixed duration. For instance, I keep most of my 1:1 meetings to thirty minutes, and if an employee needs more time, I schedule a separate session.

I introduced the reason for this when I spoke about being present. I know my limits and given my busy day anything longer than thirty minutes will be distracting because of the demands on my time. Establishing fixed duration meetings teach your employees the skills of time management and effective storytelling.

One important thing to bring up is 1:1 meetings aren't the same as your **DOOD** policy. Your DOOD policy is meant to create accessibility to leadership at any time, whereas 1:1 meetings are timely and fixed with the purpose of managing performance with intentional interaction with employees.

Resolve Roadblocks

You should use 1:1 meetings to resolve roadblocks. When it comes to work projects, assignments, or daily responsibilities, it's hard to predict what roadblocks will present themselves. Whether you have an employee who doesn't know how to kick off a project, or they're meeting resistance from stakeholders, or they just aren't getting along with peers, there are several potential stumbling blocks. You should use 1:1 meetings to identify roadblocks and help guide employees through the complexity.

Notice I didn't say you should immediately provide solutions. Effective performance management doesn't mean giving solutions. Instead, adversity should be used as an opportunity to guide your employees to resolution. Sometimes it does mean you need to insert yourself to resolve a hard roadblock, but that need not always be the go-to response. Follow-up 1:1 meetings can be used to ensure that employees have found solutions and are progressing well beyond known roadblocks by providing updates.

Updates

Updates in 1:1 meetings allow your employees to brag about themselves. When I presented the concept of cultural consequences earlier, I highlighted that some cultures have accepted norms. For the most part, especially in the United States, employees need to be encouraged to boast about their work. All too often everyone is taught to be humble or operate as a team player. While that's all fine and good, it has led to accepted marginalization.

When providing updates, employees may be reticent to speak about themselves or their accomplishments. They might believe it's better to "go along with the program" and not "stir the pot," and therefore they provide superficial work updates rather than appear self-centered and potentially be ostracized.

A successful corporate leader will know when to dig deeper and extract the facts from the employees. Ideally this would mean getting employees to boast about their work and have a sense of work ownership and pride, but it could also mean getting updates on negative interactions and progress.

Without solid updates from employees, you'll have difficulty praising a job well done or helping to resolve roadblocks. It will also be difficult to set clear expectations or to seek clarification.

Set Expectations and Seek Clarification

It should be clear by now that 1:1 meetings are all about clear communication. Along with resolving roadblocks and receiving updates, a leader can help set expectations or allow an employee to seek clarification during a 1:1 meeting.

Setting expectations is easy to understand when applied to goal setting, like SMART goals (more on this later in this chapter), but more importantly it can also be about discussing acceptable behavioral traits. If employees are expected to interact with customers in a certain way, conduct business in a particular method, or to dress in a particular fashion, 1:1 meetings are where clear expectations need to be set. There should be no surprises withheld from an employee. Instead, expectations need to be made clear from the get-go.

One important concept is all expectations need to be in line with the job description and in accordance with their compensation. I love the adage, "Early is on time, and on time is late." I get the intent of the saying, and while it's a personal motto of mine to always be early to my appointments, unless an employee is being compensated for being early, they're only expected to be "on time." I highlight this because it'd be unreasonable to set unrealistic expectations.

If you expect your employees to be fifteen minutes "early," so they can be ready to start their work, then pay them the extra fifteen minutes or shift their hours sooner to ensure the work gets done. If a person is salaried, the expectation can be different, but you need to still understand there are limits.

Remember that people work to live, they don't live to work. While there will always be exceptions, like me who can never sit still and always has something to work on, the same cannot be said for the majority.

> **When setting expectations, they should always be in line with the job description and compensation.**

When done appropriately, 1:1 meetings allow employees to seek clarification on the identified expectations. As it relates to goal setting, clarification could mean gaining insight on a deliverable or, if about behavior, providing clear work expectations. For the latter, this is extremely important if there's a counterculture within the department.

If an employee begins operating within the department but quickly realizes work and attitudes are opposite from the company's culture and contrary to a leader's expectations, then workplace roadblocks could arise. Those 1:1 meetings that create trust promote a willingness for employees to seek clarification on observed behaviors and a space for you to be open and truthful about performance.

Truthful

Your 1:1 meetings are the arena for breeding truthfulness, which is a cornerstone for creating psychological safety. I'll make one thing clear — I know there are certain things that cannot be shared with employees. When I talk about truthfulness, I'm not talking about things that must remain confidential.

By truthfulness, I mean that both employees and leaders must be willing to speak honestly and openly. For the employee this can mean being forthright about challenges in the workplace or being candid with the leader about missed opportunities or a lack of support. For the leader this can mean being upfront about expectations or being genuine when asked a career/performance question, such as identifying career stagnation.

The problem that leaders get themselves into, regarding performance management, is that some are reluctant to be truthful in their comments because they're afraid of conflict or hurt feelings. If you're leading with CARE, then you shouldn't fear hurting another person's feelings because everything you're doing is taking those feelings into consideration. It's better to be truthful at the cost of someone getting upset than it is to hide the truth and permit the loss of trust.

Early on in my management career, I didn't know how to have conversations that were truthful because of my hesitation to hurt another person's feelings. What I learned is I did more damage by withholding some truths than if I were to have been forthright in the beginning and held performance improvement conversations when necessary.

Performance Improvement Conversations

Performance improvement (PI) conversations are unique conversations because they can be uncomfortable. No one ever wants to hear that they're doing something wrong. However, if correctly approached, then performance improvement can contribute to an employee's career in conquering previous obstacles.

If you work in a large enough organization, you'll have many resources at your disposal to help you along the path of a formalized company performance improvement plan (PIP) or process. Instead of PIP, this section includes leadership practices that can be put into place when developing performance and when improvement to performance is needed or desired.

There are a few principles you should follow to ensure performance improvement conversations are **FUN**. No, I'm not making a mockery with the use of my FUN acronym. If done appropriately, you can make performance improvement conversations something that's fun for employees to do, especially when they respond positively and remedy areas of improvement.

I hope that you'll find the **FUN** in your performance improvement (PI) conversations with these three tips:

FUTURE FOCUSED

UNDERSTAND CAREER GOALS

NOT A NORMAL 1:1

Future Focused

Performance Improvement (PI) is an active process. It doesn't only occur when things are going poorly. PI conversations can be and should be future focused. Whether an employee needs to improve performance to avoid termination or is just interested in developing new skills, all conversations should be focused on the future and what can be.

> PI conversations can be seen as good or bad, but they should always be future focused.

When you identify positive behavior that exemplifies growth and demonstrates improvement, you should let an employee know with comments like, "I liked how you did X in your presentation/email/etc . . . " Then you could add to their experience by solidifying the action and connecting it to an area they're working on. That conversation would continue like, "How do you think you could apply the same technique when . . . ?"

In that way you're scaffolding their development by building off of a success. Being realistic by focusing on the future will also help employees let go of the past. When seeking PI, nothing's worse than constantly being reminded of the past when things didn't go so well.

When working with employees who want to develop new skills, avoiding career stagnation, you'd help them develop goals and opportunities that stretch their current capabilities. If your organization has annual performance targets, help your employees create goals that will allow them to work with a new set of stakeholders and potentially put them on a new career path.

Understand an Employee's Career Goals

As a manager working in several tech companies for over a decade, I've been surprised at the number of PI conversations that have helped me understand an employee's career goals. When an employee is doing well in your organization and provides insight into their career goals, it's easy to understand that a PI conversation would be smooth. What's surprised me the most is when I take time to learn the career goals of an employee who isn't performing well.

A friend of mine who works as a manager in a law enforcement dispatch center shared his frustration with one of his employees. The employee was recently off probation and had completed training successfully only to have their performance deteriorate when they were on their own. My friend was at a loss for how to address the employee's performance. I asked my friend if he knew what their employees' career goals were. He stared at me blankly and asked, "What do you mean? They're a dispatcher working for the city. I assume they just want to have a good career and solid retirement."

After some prompting, I had my friend take a different approach in his next PI meeting with the employee. A week later he called me and was dumbfounded. He learned that his employee had taken the dispatcher job because of the steady hours and benefits, but their true aspirations were to enter the medical field.

In fact, they were attending medical school a few days per week and working in the dispatch center at night. My friend and his employee were able to work out a modified schedule and a different role that both filled a need in the dispatch center and allowed his employee to meet their educational demands. After two months, the previous performance concerns were gone, and the employee was thriving.

> **When leading with CARE, you must take time to understand your employees' career goals to ensure the best possible mutual outcome.**

Don't get me wrong, sometimes accommodations can't be met, but when you know your employee's career goals you may be able to connect them with other roles and avoid career stagnation by connecting them with something that's more suitable to their skill set and better for your organization.

Not a Normal 1:1 Meeting

Lastly, and most important to note, is that PI conversations are not a normal 1:1 meeting. This isn't always obvious to leaders. Because 1:1 meetings are about TRUST, you don't want to taint the psychological safety that was built up by using that time to discuss performance improvements. You should always set aside separate meeting times to discuss PI with your employees.

We've all heard the saying, "Praise in public; correct in private." The PI conversation is a perfect venue to "correct" performance. Again, a correction in private doesn't need to be completely negative or defeating. Instead, the PI conversation can be used to realign expectations or gain additional information. It can even be used to correct something you might have done wrong as a leader. Make sure all PI conversations are separate from and in addition to 1:1 meetings.

Cognitive Load

While pursuing my doctorate at USC, I took an amazing course on learning and motivation. The course introduced a concept that transformed how I look at "workload," and that is cognitive load.

Cognitive load is the amount of information individuals can process in working memory. Working memory is often referred to as short-term memory. The idea of working memory wasn't a foreign concept to me, but what was new was learning that on average a person can only process three to five items at a time. My wonderful professor helped create a mental picture of this concept using "The Price Is Right" game of Plinko. This was further strengthened through a real-life visual example at a Google office.

Plinko is a game that has a bunch of pegs on a board, and the board sits upright. At the bottom of the board are slots with denominations, colors, or awards. You slide a disc, or chip, from the top of the board, and the disc slides down, bouncing from one peg to another until it finally settles in a slot. At the bottom of the board only one disc fits into one slot, so once it's full, nothing else fits into it.

At one of the Google offices, there was a one-story tall version of this game. You'd drop balls from the top, and as the ball progressed, a ton of flashing lights would go off as the ball bounced off pegs until it landed at the bottom.

Your working memory represents slots in a Plinko game. Once your three to five slots are filled, there's no more room in working memory. Your working memory dictates how much you can learn, process, and how well you can function daily. Let's apply this concept to employee performance.

If an employee is dealing with a relationship issue at home that's weighing on them, that takes up one slot. Let's say on the way to work they learn a loved one is in the hospital, that takes up another slot. Now they stop at their local Starbucks for a coffee. Driving out of Starbucks, back on the road, they slam on the brakes, spilling their drink in the car and on their clothes, forcing them to pull over. There goes another slot. After all those events, they end up late to work, and their colleagues are upset with them; another slot is filled.

At best they have one remaining slot after four were used up in the morning, and if they have one challenging task, difficulty, or poor interaction at work, then they'll be maxed out. All those circumstances of the day are bouncing around their minds and setting off lights and alarms, like the one-story Plinko, draining their capabilities. If this person was already a poor performer, their day is doomed to fail right from the start.

Shortly after learning about cognitive load, I was faced with a day I could feel my world falling apart, and I recognized that I'd reached my own cognitive load max.

I was on a work trip away from home when I was informed of a family member who was on the verge of succumbing to cancer. I'd woken up early to the news, and I was on the phone with my wife doing the best I could to support her and our family, but I was watching the clock because I had to leave for a meeting. When I had completed the phone call and collected my emotions, I realized I was very hungry, but all I could do was grab a protein bar for food to not delay any longer. I was able to make it to the meeting, but I was late.

After making it through my three-hour meeting, I was walking out hungrier and fully intent on grabbing food, but my phone rang; it was my wife. Fully expecting to learn about our family member, I learned that our oldest dog was debilitated.

As I spoke to my wife, I could hear our dog howling from pain in the background. Doing my best to support my wife while on the phone, I fumbled around trying to order an Uber and rushing back to my hotel room. Together we were able to convince our local vet to do a home visit.

As we were waiting for the vet, I had to take a call from my boss who was looking for volunteers to head out of the country to assist with an overseas crisis. While trying to coordinate a volunteer on my team to head out of the country, so that I wasn't voluntold, the vet finally showed up, and I had to watch virtually as our family dog was put down. All of this was going on while I was away from home, and I had my doctoral class that I couldn't miss that night.

It was one of the worst twenty-four-hour periods I had in a long time. The saving grace was I wasn't underperforming at work and had a manager fully support my need to step away. It's easy to see that on top of everything going on, if I was under work stress facing performance improvement, there's no way I would've been able to function.

As a successful corporate leader, you need to recognize when your employees are under an extreme cognitive load to be present. I'm sure you can come up with your own examples within your life when you were at your max and maybe didn't know how to put it into words. While I couldn't possibly provide an exhaustive guide to help prevent cognitive overload, I do have some tips that could help minimize its impact.

Remember that sometimes we all need understand how to **ESCAPE** a full cognitive load:

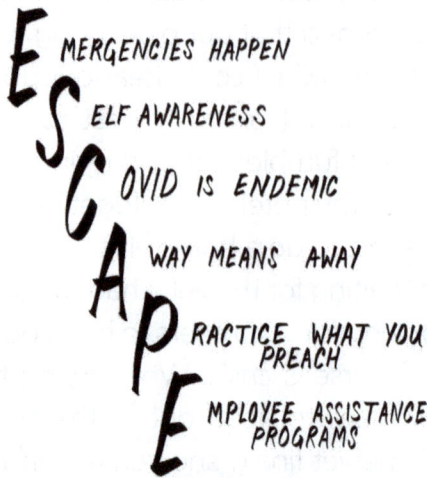

EMERGENCIES HAPPEN

SELF AWARENESS

COVID IS ENDEMIC

AWAY MEANS AWAY

PRACTICE WHAT YOU PREACH

EMPLOYEE ASSISTANCE PROGRAMS

Emergencies Happen

Emergencies happen and can take place anytime and anywhere. Make sure to demonstrate empathy for your employees and show concern when they need it. There'll always be things that pop up and are out of a person's control. It's a fact of life.

As your employees approach you to talk through their circumstances, they could be going through a gamut of emotions. The best thing you can do for them is defer judgment and provide an overwhelming amount of support. By leveraging CARE, you'll have many options to choose from to demonstrate support for your employees.

Self Awareness

Promoting mindfulness and self-awareness can help bring attention to situations that feel like they're getting out of control. It can also provide the space a person needs to reconcile what they're going through.

For leaders, this can mean exercising mindfulness through **JEMS**. For employees, it might require a leader to pull them into a last-minute meeting to have a difficult conversation and call out an elephant in the room. This should not be confrontational. Oftentimes, employees might not have any concept of what cognitive load is and may have difficulty expressing what they're going through. Having a leader privately and empathetically talking to them may be all they need to recognize what's going on. The active interest a leader exhibits in their employee's well-being may be all they need to trigger self-awareness, so they can address their needs.

COVID Is Endemic

Regardless of your own personal stance on the matter, you'll be interacting with employees who are impacted in one way or another by the unforeseen future. In the workplace, this can mean employees experiencing cognitive load when coworkers, customers, or clients cough and sneeze for something unrelated, but it immediately triggers a COVID-19 scare for employees, especially if those employees have compromised immune systems, young children, or care for others who are susceptible.

It's not your place, as a manager, to judge how an employee responds to concerns about COVID-19, the flu, or the next debilitating virus. However, it's your place to create psychologically safe environments where employees feel comfortable approaching you with concerns. This is especially important if employees are reaching their cognitive load limits.

Away Means Away

When it's time for employees to step away from work for vacation or a sick day, know that away means away. Employees work to live, not live to work. There shouldn't be demands for checking email, texts, or taking phone calls when they're off. Quite frankly if this is witnessed, then it's the leader's responsibility to step up and correct behavior. Remember that cognitive load is a real thing in the workplace and in home life. Employees don't need to worry about work while they're at home.

Practice What You Preach

As the leader, be sure to practice what you preach. In my personal example, the crisis I was experiencing wasn't over in a day. There were several days I was impacted. I took a couple days off and let my team know I was going through some difficult personal experiences and needed to step away. It was a perfect time to practice demonstrating vulnerability through **TAPE**. I made sure not to do any work and allowed myself to process all the emotions and personal circumstances that were occurring at that time in my life.

Employee Assistance Programs (EAP)

Most corporate organizations have some type of employee assistance program (EAP) and other benefits that help support an employee's well-being and improve cognitive load. Some folks feel ashamed if they need to utilize some of the EAP benefits. Ultimately, everyone could use a helping hand now and then, and EAP can be a literal life saver.

Make sure to promote EAP with your employees and support their need to take time away when a need arises. For me, this meant taking several personal leave days to regain my bearings and spend time with loved ones. If your company does not have an EAP program, you can still offer employees assistance in the way of coordinating time off, encouraging them to seek outside assistance, or just being present, practicing active listening as an employee talks.

Motivation

Motivation is the final element of performance management. As a behavior it seems like it's simple enough to understand. On the surface, motivation explains why people do what they do. However, it wasn't until my learning and motivation course at USC that I understood there was more to motivation than just "why."

Active Choice, Persistence, and Mental Effort

There are three key elements to motivation that contribute to the desire for a person to attain their goals and objectives: active choice, persistence, and mental effort. When I learned this, it was like a light bulb turned on, enlightening my own experiences.

Active Choice	the degree to which someone has the decision to pursue a goal or objective
Persistence	how hard some will continue to push when the going gets tough and explains a person's desire to accomplish the goal or objective
Mental Effort	a person's mental fortitude when dealing with ambiguity or fighting against cultural or societal norms

When you examine motivation through the framework of these three elements, it's much easier to understand how a person may or may not be invested in themselves and their work. Recently my motivation was pushed to the max when I started streaming video games as a hobby.

I have very fond memories of playing Atari and Nintendo growing up. I was lucky to have been the kid on the block that had all the newest video games and gadgets. Because of my strong connection with video games at a young age, my passion has grown into building gaming computers and learning how to stream online.

No one pushed me to learn how to stream games. I made the active choice to research how it's done and learned about the many methods like streaming from a console, single computer, or even two computers with multiple monitors. Quite frankly, I encountered so many challenges when I was learning that if it wasn't my own choice to pursue, I probably would've given up, especially when I hit speed bumps.

I was at the point where I had my two computers, one of which I built just for the purpose of streaming, set up, but I was solving new unknowns like how to make video and audio happening on one computer be captured by the other computer. Once I got the "capturing" issue solved, I had to solve how to independently control all the audio in different audio tracks, so everything sounded crisp and clean.

The mental effort of watching hundreds of hours of YouTube videos, reading dozens of websites, and trouble-shooting meant a few curse words being spewed and many late nights.

Looking back, I can say it was worth it. My systems run great, and I can stream video game play of me playing with my sons, who are scattered across the United States. The motivation for my hobby wasn't to become a famous streamer. My motivation was to be able to share with the rest of my family live memories of me and my sons playing video games.

Understanding motivation is more than knowing "why" someone does something. When you can understand the elements that contribute to motivation, you'll be able to position your employees in opportunities where they thrive. Don't get me wrong, your employees don't need to love everything they do to stay motivated and, in some cases, may never love what they do. Yet, they can remain motivated.

There are two types of motivation that are worth know-ing, extrinsic and intrinsic motivation.

Extrinsic and Intrinsic Motivation

Extrinsic motivation is based on completing a task or adhering to behavior because of an external, outside of your locus of control, punishment or reward. If an employee is stressed because they'll be late for work, then they're extrinsically motivated to get to work on time to avoid punishment. If a salesperson is constantly hustling to get customers to hit a high bonus, then they're extrinsically motivated to get the bonus as a reward. In both examples neither employee may love what they do — well maybe the salesperson loves the money — but nevertheless they're motivated to get to work on time and get top sales. On the flip side, there's intrinsic motivation.

Intrinsic motivation is performing a task because it's personally rewarding. An employee at a coffee shop who decides to learn sign language even though it's not required is intrinsically motivated because it's rewarding to communicate with customers who are deaf or hard of hearing. A salesperson who volunteers their time to guide consumers in credit repair is intrinsically motivated because it'd be rewarding to help others secure their financial future.

Often, if a person is intrinsically motivated, they love what they do. Every one of us experiences intrinsic motivation daily. Just look at your hobbies. You have a hobby because it's what you love to do. Some people repair and ride motorcycles, while others collect stamps, and some of us build computers to play games. Of the two, intrinsic motivation is the best for sustaining interest in the long run. How many of your hobbies have outlasted your jobs or even relationships?

When you understand how motivation works, you'll have a better chance of managing employee performance in the long run. You don't always need to have your employees love what they do to be successful. However, if you need to help improve an employee's performance, finding the right motivation could make all the difference in the world.

Key Takeaways

1 Productive 1:1 meetings are focused on **TRUST**: they should be timely and occur at regular intervals, focus on resolving roadblocks, allow time for employees to give updates (especially when something has gone well), allow leaders to set expectations and employees to seek clarification, and embrace truthfulness to create psychological safety.

2 Performance improvement conversations should be **FUN**: future focused, enable you to understand an employee's career goals, and not done during a normal 1:1 meeting.

3 Cognitive load is the amount of information individuals can process in working memory. You can't know everything someone is carrying in their cognitive load, but you can recognize when employees might be carrying more than usual.

4 We all need to know how to **ESCAPE** a full cognitive load: Emergencies happen; demonstrate empathy and show concern for employees when they need it. When it's time for employees to step away from work, know that away means away. Encourage employees to make use of the EAP, and if your company doesn't have one, work with them to coordinate time off, provide accommodations, or encourage them to seek outside assistance. As the leader, be sure to practice what you preach.

5 Active choice is the degree to which someone has the decision to pursue a goal or objective. Persistence determines how hard some will continue to push when the going gets tough. Mental effort will determine a person's mental fortitude when dealing with ambiguity or fighting against cultural or societal norms.

6 Extrinsic motivation is completing a task or adhering to behavior because of an external, outside of your locus of control, punishment or reward. Intrinsic motivation is performing a task because it's personally rewarding.

Chapter 13:
Performance Enablement

Performance enablement may be relatively new for some people. I define performance enablement as proactively and intentionally investing in people, so they bring their best selves to work. I've discussed ad nauseum that successful corporate leadership requires intentional action on the part of the leader. However, in my experience and in my education, there isn't enough emphasis on the elements associated with explaining intentional and active leadership.

Performance Development	
Performance Management (Employee-Centric)	**Performance Enablement (Leader-Centric)**
• 1:1 meetings • Performance improvement • Cognitive load • Motivation	• Performance review • Understanding human capital • Growth vs. fixed mindset • SMART goals

You can find many programs that focus on performance management. After all, it's the area that focuses on the employee's performance. However, as I proposed in my EVOC example: why do we only blame the employee, and not the manager when things go awry? I see performance enablement as focusing on the leader's contributions and how they can modify their actions and thought processes when interacting with employees, lending to their long-term performance development.

Performance enablement can be as dependable as **PUGS**:

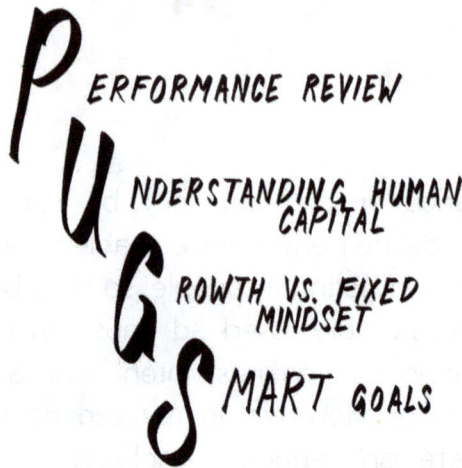

PERFORMANCE REVIEW

UNDERSTANDING HUMAN CAPITAL

GROWTH VS. FIXED MINDSET

SMART GOALS

Like elements of performance management, some of the elements of performance enablement might overlap with one another, but it's important to understand the nuances between each.

Performance Review

Performance review is a regular process, often completed annually, in most corporations in which performance is rated on a formal scale. The process provides an employee with an understanding of how well they're performing against job expectations and role scope. A successful corporate leader should always have regular performance conversations, so employees always know where they stand, and there are no surprises. The formalized performance review process allows a leader to document successes, highlight strengths, and to identify areas of opportunities.

There are way too many different types of performance review processes to discuss here, but one thing they all have in common is all employees are reviewed in a company. It's the one time per year when your employees are the focus, and their contributions can be highlighted to take center stage. I personally enjoy the performance review process, but many overlook the value it provides to performance enablement.

The performance review process is the ultimate way a leader can serve as an ally (see **Chapter 10: Providing Leadership with Realism**). Often your employees won't understand the amount of time and effort you'll exert in the review process, but that's not the point. As a selfless act, you'll be able to advocate for your employees when considering high ratings that could later determine raises, bonuses, and even career advancement.

As an element of performance enablement, this is where all your previous efforts culminate to ensure an equitable and transparent rating of your employees. Depending on your organization, appropriate and fair ratings can either set up your employees on a successful career path or hinder their growth leading to a **GAG** environment.

Understanding Human Capital

Some readers might be wondering how human capital can be an element of performance enablement. Human capital refers to the knowledge, skills, and experience an employee brings to the organization. Over time leaders forget their employees are more than numbers on a page or part of a "headcount" in an organization.

Day in and day out your employees are fulfilling a role within your company or department, and they're using their toolkit of knowledge, skills, and experience to create impact over time. That impact adds up to an incredible amount of institutional knowledge.

I've been part of my fair share of reduction in force and department reorgs in which the human element of human capital is forgotten. There tends to be a belief in some corporate environments that it's easier to replace employees with more experienced or "seasoned" professionals than it is to invest in your staff that's already contributing to impact.

There'll always be a case made to terminate some non-performers. But for those motivated to leverage their skills for the betterment of the company or department, they require a successful corporate leader to step up to the plate and enable them to demonstrate their value.

Countless articles and studies advocate internal employee investment over hiring new employees. Not only is there an economical value add of performance enablement for internal employees, but there's also that notion of motivation and cognitive load (see **Chapter 12: Performance Management**).

By finding the appropriate level of motivation for your employees and managing their cognitive load, they'll be able to utilize their toolkit to its maximum. You lose a lot of time, commitment, energy, and workplace investment when you replace an employee with a new person.

The one exception is if you must hire an external person because you don't have the skill set among internal employees. However, once that type of person is hired, you can increase the capital of your organization by allowing stretch assignments where existing personnel are able to learn new skills from the new hire, thereby improving succession planning.

Ultimately, the leader is the one who must enable performance, improving the capital of their organization and recognizing their employees are more than numbers on a page.

Growth Mindset vs. Fixed Mindset

Having a fixed mindset is simply believing that intelligence is static, meaning that there is only so much intelligence a person will ever have and can ever have. Growth mindset is the opposite and views intelligence as something that can be developed over time. I'll be honest; the first time I heard about growth mindset I didn't understand the hoopla.

A Meta colleague gave a presentation on the difference between growth and fixed mindsets. It seemed straightforward and simple enough to me. As I looked at the more junior employees in the room, I could see the information start to resonate. Then I heard the behavioral traits associated with each, and I knew there was value for us to understand the differences between the two.

In my studies, I've had an opportunity to dig deeper identifying the differences and wished I'd known more about the two types of mindsets earlier in my management career. Broken down in the following chart you can see a drastic difference in behavior between a growth versus fixed mindset when facing adversity.

Behavioral Differences between Growth vs. Fixed Mindset

Growth	Fixed
• Views feedback as an opportunity • Inspired by others' success • Embraces challenges • Willing to adapt and make changes	• Views feedback as an attack • Threatened by others' success • Avoids challenges • Stubborn and reticent to changes

It's important for you as a successful corporate leader to recognize the two mindsets, so you can adapt your leadership style to accommodate your employees. I'm not saying you need to be inauthentic, but you need to learn how to customize your message based on who you're talking to.

Based on the behavioral differences listed in the chart, those employees who embrace a growth mindset would be better prepared to handle adversity. In a perfect world a successful corporate leader would be able to shift the thinking of those with a fixed mindset to a growth mindset. While this could be a worthwhile endeavor, it shouldn't be entirely up to the leader to decide. Remember that mindset is an element within performance enablement. A leader would need to identify where the mindset of their employee lies and then enable them to succeed regardless of the type.

I have some tips that can help **CRAFT** a positive environment, enabling those with either a growth or fixed mindset to succeed:

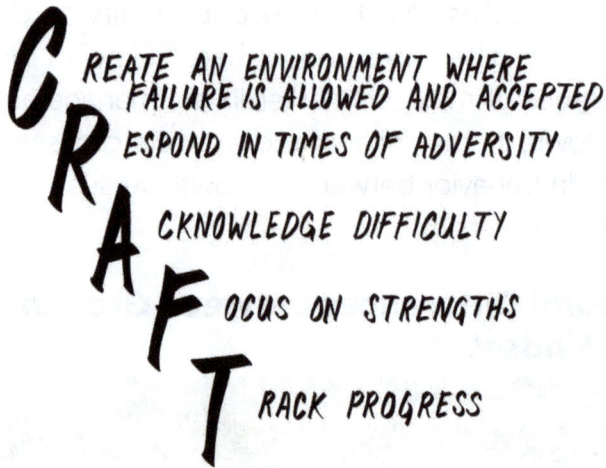

C REATE AN ENVIRONMENT WHERE FAILURE IS ALLOWED AND ACCEPTED

R ESPOND IN TIMES OF ADVERSITY

A CKNOWLEDGE DIFFICULTY

F OCUS ON STRENGTHS

T RACK PROGRESS

Create an Environment Where Failure Is Allowed and Accepted

There will always be exceptions for violations of codes of conduct, but aside from extreme behavioral fouls, workplace failure needs to be part of the culture. Especially useful for those with a fixed mindset, a culture that learns from failure will leave little room for self-doubt and fear of challenges.

At one point, one of Meta's mottos was, "Move fast and break things." The problem was too many people over embraced "break things," so they had to change it to, "Move fast together."

The point of the original motto was to not be afraid of failure. As leaders we fear making mistakes (by now you should feel off the hook for this one) and play it safe. That type of fixed mindset does not allow for innovation and growth.

While at Meta, I failed to fully embrace **CARE** for one of my employees. I was afraid to hurt an employee's feelings by calling out some serious missed opportunities. Ultimately, that employee took work leave and, after a few months, voluntarily left the company. I was in a debrief with my manager Mary Jane after the fact, and I fully thought she was going to read me the riot act for my failure. Instead, Mary Jane opened the conversation with a simple question, "What did you learn from this?" Knowing I was already being hard on myself, instead of berating me for a failure, Mary Jane forced me to learn something from it.

Had Mary Jane taken a different approach, I would've missed the opportunity to learn from my mistake. Supporting a growth mindset approach, not berating an employee, and pivoting the focus as a learning opportunity will create space to grow from the experience.

Respond in Times of Adversity

When notified of times employees are facing adversity, it's the leader's responsibility to respond. Like in the breakdown of 1:1 meetings, adversity should be used as an opportunity to help guide your employees to resolution. Regarding mindset, times of crisis should be used as opportunities to offer support.

Acknowledge Difficulty

The first way to offer support is to acknowledge the person's difficulty. This doesn't necessarily mean to validate the difficulty. There may be a time and place for that, but it's not here. It also doesn't mean diminishing the difficulty. Instead, this is a perfect time to express empathy. After all, what one person views as difficult may be a walk in a park to another, but it doesn't make it any less difficult to the person in crisis.

Focus on Strengths

Once a leader has acknowledged the difficulty, it creates a great opportunity to focus on the person's strengths. The proper mindset can be a powerful tool, and it can make all the difference in the world. Particularly when dealing with people with a fixed mindset, the best way to get employees out of a rut is to help them focus on their strengths.

Track Progress

Maybe your employee is facing challenges because they lack skills in a particular area. By having them focus on their strengths, you can help identify opportunities and remove obstacles for them by partnering them with a colleague to shore up their weaknesses. Once you have them back on track, you can hold follow up meetings to track progress through your 1:1 meetings.

It's sad to say but the reality is if you're a leader with a fixed mindset, you're in for a struggle. To be successful, you need to modify your actions and thought processes when interacting with employees, lending to their long-term performance development. Remember the key to appropriate performance enablement is for you as the leader to focus on your behaviors and actions, responding to your employees needs and positioning them for success.

Our world is always changing and our need to adapt and remain nimble as leaders is paramount. A few years ago, COVID-19 wasn't even on the radar, but the pandemic turned the office environment upside down. The hybrid workplace has become more commonplace and the "water cooler" now exists in the cloud through virtual meeting spaces. Leaders possessing a growth mindset are more important now than ever before.

SMART Goals

Documented goals go a long way in establishing clear expectations and holding others accountable for performance. A widely known concept nowadays, George T. Doran first introduced a SMART way to write management goals and objectives (Doran, 1981).

The easiest and most efficient way to create a goal is ensuring it's **SMART**:

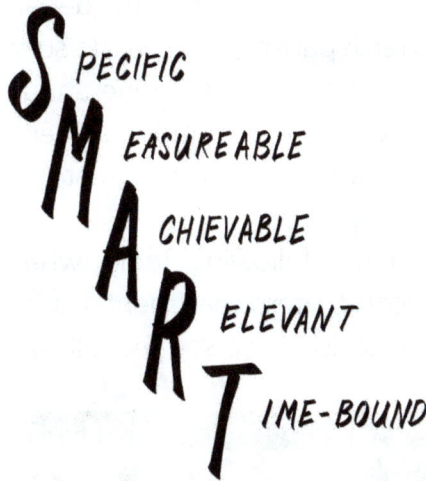

SPECIFIC

MEASUREABLE

ACHIEVABLE

RELEVANT

TIME-BOUND

When applied to goal setting, you want to set specific goals for your employees. There needs to be a way to measure success. They can't be so obnoxious that they're impossible to attain, so they need to be achievable. They need to be relevant to the employee's job, or in the case of a stretch assignment relevant to employee's growth, and the company. There needs to be a time-bound completion date, so you can measure progress.

There are an infinite number of examples we can come up with on how SMART goals can play out in the workplace. As a method of performance enablement, a leader has the responsibility to ensure established SMART goals contribute to the overall company VMOs, as well as the employee's development. The rub is sometimes company and department SMART goals aren't so smart. I witnessed this phenomenon in my first year at Google.

Google has an annual company survey called Googlegeist that measures employee satisfaction in a variety of areas. The survey is thorough, and managers get a full, anonymous, breakdown of the results complete with year-over-year comparisons and comments.

When I took over leadership of my department, I learned about another interdepartmental specific survey that was like Googlegeist. The survey was also done annually and within a month or two of Googlegeist. The department survey seemed redundant to me, and I went to great lengths to assess its validity.

Illustrated in the following table, when reviewing the reason for the second interdepartmental survey and applying a SMART goals breakdown we see the following:

Interdepartmental Survey		
Goal	Condition Satisfied	How
Specific	✓	Measure employee satisfaction
Measurable	✓	Percentage of responses and change year over year
Achievable	✓	Delivered annually
Relevant	✓	Provided metrics on department health
Time-bound	✓	Employees given two weeks to complete

Clearly the interdepartmental survey checked all the boxes and was in fact a SMART goal, but in the end, it wasn't so smart. When I compared the data, comments, and number of responses between the interdepartmental survey and Googlegeist, the differences were negligible. If anything, since my department had their own survey, the logistics and workload to launch, aggregate, and present the data was an illogical burden. After the first year of going through the experience myself, I quickly canceled the survey and relied solely on the company's Googlegeist.

I don't think that leaders spend enough time asking themselves or their employees if they should be working on certain goals. We all get caught up in our day-to-day work, and sometimes our intrinsic motivation guides us toward creating a new SMART goal because it seems brighter and shinier than what we need to be working on.

The times our best intentions lead us astray are when the successful corporate leader needs to step in, reprioritize, and redirect focus. By ensuring SMART goals are aligned appropriately, a leader can position their employees in a way that maximizes their efficiency, contributing to impact that supports the company and department.

I learned the whole purpose behind the interdepartmental survey was to measure job satisfaction and create new training opportunities using feedback. Since we had all the information needed from Googlegeist, we could've chosen to implement solutions rather than waste energy duplicating efforts and gathering more data without taking corrective action.

SMART goals that could've been created to improve job satisfaction and create new training opportunities, meeting the initial desired goal, include:

- **Every quarter provide employees with two-hour refresher training in one of the following areas: project management, data collection, strategic**

thinking, or data analysis, ensuring at least eighty percent employee attendance.

- **Every quarter host voluntary one-hour-long brown bag lunches with stakeholders from facilities, real estate, finance, and operations to speak about open opportunities, targeting fifty percent employee attendance.**

As you can see in the examples provided, SMART goals don't need to be a heavy burden. They're a simple method of formatting expectations. The trick is if one element is missing, then you could miss out on full accountability.

For example, if you don't bind an expectation with a time, you'll be subject to the employee's timeline. This could be problematic for a leader depending on a specific outcome to occur by a specific date.

If you forget to specify something that can be measured, you'll have no way of quantifying success or failure. For SMART goals to be effective, all elements must be present when documenting expectations.

You can't be effective if you aren't realistic about your own abilities or the abilities of your employees. Having CARE means not being afraid to address the hard stuff and everything a successful corporate leader does is for the benefit of their employees.

Key Takeaways

1 The formalized performance review process allows you to document successes, highlight strengths, and identify areas of opportunity. It's the ultimate way a leader can serve as an ally. Considering high ratings that could later determine raises, bonuses, and even career advancement, performance reviews enable you to advocate for your employees among peers and to senior leadership.

2 Human capital refers to the knowledge, skills, and experience an employee brings to the organization. Employees who are motivated to leverage their skills for the betterment of the organization require a successful corporate leader to step up and enable them to demonstrate their value.

3 While extrinsic motivation serves its purpose in specific situations, intrinsic motivation is the best for sustaining interest and commitment in the long run.

4 A growth mindset views intelligence as something that can be developed over time. Having a growth mindset makes you better prepared to handle adversity.

5 **SMART** goals should be specific, measurable, achievable, relevant, and time-bound. You have a responsibility to ensure established SMART goals contribute to the overall company VMOs, as well as the employee's development.

Express Empathy:
Communication

It sounds silly to some, but I like to remind my team that words have meaning. You may be turning up an eyebrow and thinking, with such profound insight it's a wonder I didn't have a book published sooner. The reality is we all forget how powerful words can be.

I run a podcast called *Ely's Echo*. In that podcast I've revealed meaningful and personal information through stories from my life. In one of my stories, I explain how I grew up knowing what it was like to be hungry.

For a portion of my life as a young adult, there were times when finances were few, and food was scarce. As an only child, it got to the point where I would save food when eating at homes of friends or family members, so I could bring leftovers home to my mother.

As a by-product of those low times growing up, my wife and sons know that I'll never say that I am "starving." I learned what being "very hungry" meant, but I know even in the worst of times, I was never starving. Yet, you hear it all the time. People nowhere close to starving will use "starving" as their adjective, when what they mean is they're only "hungry."

I don't begrudge those who use the word starving. Instead, I point out that people have forgotten that words have meaning and have become disconnected with the impact of certain words.

The words you use daily can give power or take it away. When coupled with a communication style, effectively using the right words at the right time to show concern can lend to your authenticity as a leader and help you express empathy.

Why Empathy?

The first step to understanding empathy is understanding the impact words have or don't have when used insincerely. Empathy is the ability to sense or understand what another person is thinking, experiencing, or feeling without being told. It's mandatory for a successful corporate leader to understand how to express empathy. It's so important that it's the final letter in the acronym **CARE**, saving the best for last.

The people you'll be leading are more than numbers on a page, or part of a headcount in a company or department. They're a collective of human capital bringing their knowledge, skills, and experience with them to the workplace. They also contribute to the living, breathing culture that's at the heart of all their interactions. Empathy means caring about those in your charge both as a whole and individually. It doesn't mean you need to become best friends forever, but it does mean acknowledging the lived experience your people bring with them to the workplace. That lived experience will manifest in many ways. Sometimes it will be good, and your employees will flourish. Other times, it won't be so good, and they'll falter.

Empathy is a required skill that will allow you to consider and attempt to understand what another person is going through. When you can understand how another person might be feeling, and you understand how words can lift them up or tear them down, you can adjust your communication style to have great impact on their success and yours.

Chapter 14: Communication Styles

Knowing how to express empathy with proper communication is the most important skill a successful corporate leader can employ. I'm such an advocate and firm believer in perfecting communication that my bachelor's degree, master's degree, and doctorate degree all focus on communication in one way, shape, or form.

While I've spent the greater part of a decade working on improving my ability to effectively communicate, sometimes I feel like I'm getting no better at it because of its complexity. However, it's such an essential skill that I'll never stop working on improving my ability.

Four commonly understood styles of communication are:
- **Passive**
- **Aggressive**
- **Passive-aggressive**
- **Assertive**

Regardless of the style you choose to use, or your employees use, as a successful corporate leader you should practice assuming best intentions.

Assume Best Intentions

The same way I don't assume that employees wake up every day intent on being awful at their job, so too I don't assume that people choose to communicate a message poorly. I always assume best intent when a person's communicating a message — especially if they're using a low-context method like email.

Effective communication can be difficult, and outside of specific adversarial conditions, I like to give the sender the benefit of the doubt as I receive their message. As I practice, I encourage a successful corporate leader to employ the same manner of acceptance. Assuming best intent will go a long way for dealing with the variety of communication styles.

Passive Communication

A passive communication style is one in which the communicator avoids confrontation, eye contact, and can seem to go with the flow. Often weary of drawing attention to themselves and hesitant to be in the limelight, I find passive communicators some of the more difficult to deal with, because you seldom know where they really stand. Since they're reluctant to cause a fuss, they'll often be agreeable because they're so reluctant to cause a confrontation or say "no." These types of communicators are overly apologetic (saying "sorry" way too often).

In workplace environments where the tasks are pre-dictable and status quo is the preferred method of execution, passive communicators may be a boon, but in dynamic environments it'd be like pulling teeth to learn how a passive communicator really feels. The best way to handle this type of communication style is to ask open-ended questions and be as direct as possible in 1:1 meetings.

If you're a passive communicator in a leadership position, you need to explore other communication styles and develop a growth mindset to implement tactics from other styles (see **Chapter 13: Performance Enablement**). A passive communicator will be so preoccupied trying to make everyone happy and maintain an easygoing attitude that employees will take advantage, and all semblance of leadership and management will be lost.

Aggressive Communication

Quite the opposite of passive, aggressive communicators attempt to dominate every conversation they're in. Over-valuing their own opinion, they're quick to interrupt others and exaggerate nonverbal communication with the use of gestures and intense eye contact.

Aggressive communicators aren't afraid to speak their mind at the expense of others. This type of communication style can be seen as counterproductive in some workplace environments but may flourish in others. Reluctant to apologize for anything, aggressive communicators will have an overbearing personality. They'll be ready to speak their mind without regard for others around them.

The best way to deal with aggressive communicators is to be mindful of them and not allow yourself to be roped in. Maintaining clear deliberate conversations while remaining calm and present will set you up for success. The most important thing is to always remain professional even if verbally assaulted with personal insults.

If you're an aggressive communicator and are in a leadership position, you'll have a very difficult time forming strong relationships with your employees. You'll need to make a conscious effort to suppress your aggressive tendencies when dealing with your employees. Using the methods outlined in *Lead with CARE* will help you connect with others but only if aggressive communication methods can be tempered.

Passive-Aggressive Communication

The passive-aggressive communication style is the most precarious. This type of communicator will be passive on the surface, but deep down they're aggressive. Passive-aggressive communicators often make snide remarks about others indirectly and relish in sarcasm. Some of the worst behaviors of those who communicate this way occur when they seem happy go lucky on the surface but are ready to undermine authority at the most opportune moment.

The best way to deal with this type of communicator is to call out the behavior when you see it and to be as direct as possible, leaving no room for interpretation. In my opinion, passive-aggressive communicators have difficulty communicating their thoughts and processing their emotions. By being direct and soliciting their feedback in a private setting, you may be able to dismantle their passive-aggression.

If you're a passive-aggressive communicator in a leadership position, focus on creating environments of trust and regularly leveraging **JEMS** to control your emotions. Once in control of your emotions, you'll need to focus on productively sharing your thoughts while being considerate of others. Like with aggressive communication, all is not lost if you're a passive-aggressive communicator, but intentionally focusing on how messages get communicated is a must.

Assertive Communication

Assertive communication is the most productive. Maintaining a balance of respect and collaboration, assertive communicators are confident in expressing their thoughts and ideas. Assertive communicators are good at making others feel comfortable and are friendly in their approach. You don't need any special skills when dealing with assertive communicators. In fact, highly productive assertive communicators can be encouraged to share ideas. Enlist them for their assistance in partnering with communicators of the other communication styles.

If you're an assertive communicator in a leadership position, you're off to a good start when it comes to expressing empathy. In fact, understanding and sharing feelings with others will probably come naturally to you.

Key Takeaways

1	Always assume best intent when a person is communicating a message — especially if they're using a low-context method like email.
2	Passive communicators avoid confrontation, so it can be difficult to know where they stand. Ask open-ended questions and be as direct as possible in 1:1 meetings. If you're a passive communicator, consider implementing elements of other styles to avoid losing authority among your team.
3	Aggressive communicators try to dominate every conversation and may be overbearing. Don't let yourself get roped in by them. Remain calm and professional. Having an aggressive communication style can make it difficult to build strong relationships with employees, so learn to temper your communication and explore methods to connect with others.
4	Passive-aggressive communicators may seem passive on the surface but can be aggressive deep down. They often use sarcasm and have difficulty communicating their thoughts and processing emotions. In a private setting, try to reach them by being direct and soliciting their feedback. If you're a passive-aggressive communicator, focus on creating environments of trust, understanding your emotions (try **JEMS**), and productively sharing your thoughts.
5	Assertive communicators maintain a balance of respect and collaboration. They're good at making others feel comfortable and are friendly in their approach.

Chapter 15: Communication Methods

Communication style is one half of the recipe for expressing empathy with communication. The other half is the method. Communication methods are vast and consist of a variety of elements. The concept of communication is so easy to grasp that it's often overlooked as a skill. Understanding the transactional process that occurs as two parties, or sender-receiver binary, send and receive information across a medium is essential in the communication process. If that explanation were enough for everyone to be a successful corporate leader, I'd stop right there, but that's only the tip of the iceberg.

Noise in Communication

The transactional process, or give and take, that occurs as messages are sent and received is where noise gets intermixed and where misunderstandings are introduced in all forms of communication. There are a handful of commonly identified types of noise (see table on the next page).

Semantic and physical noise are easily identified, and we can all recall examples in which they disrupted and derailed conversations. Physiological and psychological are easy to identify in us, with a few exceptions, but are extremely hard to identify in others. For example, it's not always easy to identify when someone has a headache or is in emotional distress. Regardless of whether we can identify them, you must know the four types of noise can sabotage a message, allowing it to be distorted and received differently than expected.

Semantic	Semantic noise occurs commonly when someone isn't proficient in a language. It can also occur when people use industry jargon not commonly known.
Physical	Physical noise has to do with environmental sounds, like trying to talk at a concert or when there's inclement weather like a windstorm.
Physiological	Physiological noise is commonly overlooked and associated with the physical factors someone is experiencing like a headache or the flu. Physiological noise is important to understand because it impacts a person's cognitive load.
Psychological	Psychological noise includes the mental and emotional barriers that impact a person. Imposter syndrome (which we discussed in **Chapter 8: Common Pitfalls to Avoid**) and heavy cognitive loads would fall into this category.

Impact of Medium and Context in Communication

To add even more complexity, consider how messages are received differently depending on the chosen medium. For example, one message received in person could be perceived much differently if sent by text or email. An easy way to understand this is to think back to a circumstance when you received a text message from a significant other and were immediately put off, only to find out you completely misunderstood the meaning. Let me give you an innocent example that happened to me.

My wife and I are empty nesters with four boys out of the house, and after a year of it being just the two of us at home, we're still working out our routine. The night before trash day my wife reminded me to put the trash out. As an early riser, the following morning I put the trash cans out on the street and left for work.

Later that day, my wife sent me what I thought was a saying, "Thanks for putting the trash out!" I responded with a heart emoji and a simple, "You're welcome." She then responded with a message that totally threw me for a loop — "Next time, I'll just do it myself." I was totally taken aback.

After several more text messages that only furthered our confusion, I made it home from work and we both realized the miscommunication. When my wife asked me to put the trash out, in her mind she was referring to the full trash bag in the kitchen, knowing trash day was coming.

I didn't realize the kitchen trash needed to go out, so I just put the cans on the street. It's obvious how the text messages went downhill from there as my wife was trying to be sarcastic, and I thought she was being sincere. In the end, we were both right and both wrong, but the medium we were communicating through, in this case text messages, didn't do us any favors. It took a discussion in person to iron out all the details.

Know that depending on your chosen medium of communication (see some examples and their drawbacks later in this chapter), you may leave room for misunderstandings and/or misinterpretations to creep in. Be sure to be intentional about your chosen method, and based on the circumstances ensure you choose something that allows you to maximize how you express empathy.

Closely associated with cultural consciousness (discussed in **Chapter 5: Diversity, Equity, and Inclusion (DEI)**) is recognizing the difference between low-context and high-context cultures. Depending on the cultural context of two people communicating, you might be forced into only one preferred method of communication, such as face-to-face, to reduce semantic misunderstanding.

The United States is a low-context culture, meaning communication is direct and to-the-point, attempting to leave no margin for interpretation. Japan is a high-context culture relying heavily on implied understanding rather than explicit understanding. A high-context culture depends heavily on nonverbal communication and shared meaning.

When it comes time to blend communicators from each context together, if neither is prepared to interpret the context based on the culture where the other is from, then it could lead to frustrating outcomes. Recall the story of my partnership with someone who was native to China. Had I not taken time to understand the cultural context of my colleague, work delays and shortcomings could have continued.

Verbal and Nonverbal Communication

There are two primary forms that communication can take on, verbal and nonverbal. "Official" studies are all over the board on the percentage of communication that's nonverbal. One study says 55 percent, another says 80 percent, and yet another says 93 percent.

We can assume at least 50 percent of communication is nonverbal. That's still a lot of nonverbal communication going on. From this baseline we can all agree that being able to pick up on nonverbal cues during a conversation would be very valuable, especially when communicating within a high-context culture.

Nonverbal cues can consist of body language, eye contact, facial expression, gestures, noises, posture, and proximity. Understanding nonverbal cues will allow you to get a "read" on a person. You'll be able to understand if their verbal communication aligns with what you're seeing.

For instance, is your significant other saying they're fine if you go out with your friends, but their gestures and facial expressions say otherwise? Does an employee on your team say they're confident they'll meet a deadline, but their body language and avoidance of eye contact convey a lack of confidence? Understanding the importance of verbal and nonverbal cues is a great skill for a successful corporate leader to possess.

In all instances with a potential for miscommunication due to the context or medium used, the best thing to do is slow down and ask for clarity when needed. You can depend on nonverbal communication to help solidify your understanding of a message.

Be an Active Listener

Active listening is a skill that can make the difference between a good or great successful corporate leader. Think of active listening as the lens with which you'll evaluate all verbal and nonverbal communication.

By implementing five easy steps, active listening will be like taking a walk through the **PARCS**:

PRESENT

ATTENTIVE

REFLECT

CLARIFY

SUMMARIZE

Present

When you're present (listed as a skill again) and engaged in active listening, you're filtering out your own physiological and psychological barriers, so you can be completely invested as you interact with your employees. Whether it's a presentation, group meeting, or 1:1 meeting, you need to be sure you're not allowing yourself to be distracted, so that your team or individual employees recognize how much you value their contributions.

Attentive

Being attentive goes beyond just listening. Exercising attentiveness means taking in the entire picture. Active listening is the lens you'll use to examine verbal and nonverbal communication, attentiveness is how.

You are registering the words being said, how they're being said, and the method in which they're being used. You're also watching to ensure that the nonverbal cues you see align with the message. All of this is being done while you're listening to understand. Listening to understand is the act of being so attentive that you fully comprehend what the other person is saying.

> **If you're thinking about how you're going to respond to something, are you really listening to what that person is saying?**

Reflect

Reflecting on what you heard is a key component of listening to understand. I once worked with a human resource representative who said, "You should always listen to understand and not to reload." Think of it this way: if you've ever had an argument with anyone, you probably held the position that everything you said was right, and everything the other person said was wrong.

In that type of one-sided "conversation," can you reflect now and recognize that you were probably "reloading" a response to fire back at the other person? We do it all the time. When we get so emotionally charged that we're going to prove we're right no matter what, we'll hear something the other person says and then stop listening because we're preparing this amazing, well-formatted retort that requires all our attention.

If we're truly attentive, we lay our emotions off to the side and can listen for reflection rather than reloading. When we reflect on what's being said, rather than listening to retort, we can paraphrase what we hear to make sure we understand what the other person is attempting to convey. Reflection can be a powerful leadership skill, but what it does for others is amazing. When you can accurately paraphrase the other persons' point even if they were heated and attempting to lure you into a debate, it disarms them because they realize you were present, attentive, and listening to understand their perspective.

Clarify

You aren't infallible, but that's where clarity comes into play. In the transactional process of communication, some-times no matter how hard you try details will slip past you, or you'll zone out when valuable information is passing you by. It happens. Being able to correctly pause someone's dialogue to seek clarity on an important issue is a requirement of effective active listening.

When you're in the middle of an important conversation with an employee, while it may feel uncomfortable, it's acceptable to politely interject for clarity. Pausing a person's explanation, especially when it could mean understanding a very valuable element, is better than having the employee carry on only for you to end up lost or confused and completely missing the point.

We all have moments we rattle things off so quickly that even the most adept listener couldn't keep up. Maybe there's an issue of semantics, and something is said that you aren't familiar with or could potentially misconstrue. Seeking clarity on ambiguous items, or to ensure you have a clear understanding, is an acceptable practice. If done right, it conveys to the other person that you want to fully understand what they're talking about.

Summarize

When the conversation is ending, summarize all the key takeaways. This could be you summarizing all the highlights you heard. It could also be the other person summarizing what they heard.

Providing space for both parties to share their understanding will help alleviate the potential for a misunderstanding down the line. While it's situation-dependent, you could also summarize after the fact with an email. Be careful with how you summarize, and how often, since follow-up emails are a method for performance improvement and could be construed as something negative rather than a method of positive affirmation.

Communication Mediums

How you choose to communicate a message will depend on, among other things, the message itself. I had a manager who once said, "An email should be neutral at worst." One step further we can make the statement even more understandable by saying, "Anything negative taking written form should always be conveyed neutrally."

If you have something awful, rude, or hurtful to say, or if your emotions are at their max, don't write anything worse than something neutral. We've all seen, heard of, read, or been party to receiving a hurtful message. Once something is written down and sent there's no taking it back.

For leaders, this is extremely important to understand. I've been hot under the collar more than a few times, and I can recall those moments when I wrote an email but was smart enough to leave it in draft form. I practiced **JEMS** by stepping away from the draft for a full day and implemented mindfulness. I returned to it only to delete the draft and rewrite something that was amicable.

You can allow yourself to experience hurt or anger, but as a successful corporate leader you let it go. Another option some people forget about is talking through the situation with the other person over a phone call, video conference, or in person if you can do so calmly. Regardless of how you choose to communicate, don't let your emotions get the best of you.

Broken down in the following chart are some common communication mediums along with their benefits and drawbacks. Each has its place, and each won't be useful all the time, but understanding their benefits and drawbacks will help you realize their potential.

Common Communication Mediums

	Benefit	Drawback
Face-to-Face	• It's personal • Easier to read verbal and nonverbal cues • Great for direct feedback	• Requires being in the office • Sometimes difficult for employee to feel psychologically safe • Could be difficult for some employees to express their feelings

	Benefit	Drawback
Video Call	• Can be done anywhere • Could assist with location and proximity challenges • Can support an individual or several people • Could help employees communicate easier if they're anxious in person	• Can feel impersonal • Harder to pick up on nonverbal cues • If too many people are on, then not everyone may have a voice • Opens the door for technical issues
Email	• Easy to send from anywhere to anyone • Easier to ensure complex tasks are well outlined • A globally acceptable method of communication • Serves as creating a virtual paper trail	• It's impersonal • Sometimes hard for employees to manage work/life balance because emails can be checked on a mobile device • Can lead to micromanaging because of the ease of sending messages • Once something is sent, it's very difficult (if not impossible) to retract
All Hands (Dept. Meetings)	• Great for sending one mass announcement to many people at once • Creates transparency • If combined with video conference, then can assist with location/ proximity challenges • Grabs everyone's attention for a short time	• Messages tend to be vague and generically designed for masses • Provides no sense of individuality • More difficult for some employees to feel individually supported
Newsletter	• Great for sending a mass announcement to many people at once • Easy way to document ongoings • Great way to provide large-scale recognition	• It's another task that employees need to spend time on to get information • Not personalized • Depending on the size of an organization it can show favoritism if the same team, group, or people are regularly receiving attention

Of the many communication mediums listed above, you won't use every single one all the time. Communication is a two-way street. Just as it's important for you to identify your preferred method of communication, so too must you identify how your employees prefer to communicate. When I meet a new team member or take over a new department, I spend time introducing myself, and I explain my preferred method of contact. For me it's: email, text, phone call — in that order. For standard day-to-day needs, business email is the way to go. If the matter requires faster attention or a quick response, text is up next. Finally, if the matter is sensitive, urgent, or needs immediate response, a phone call is required.

I've been amazed at the response I get from my employees when I explain how best to communicate with me because other leaders hadn't been so forthright. Having clear communication channels established with your team is a great way to illustrate empathy because it lets your team know you're available to them when they need you.

The pendulum does swing the other way. You need to elicit from your employees how they prefer to communicate. In this way you can empower them by seeking their input and not making assumptions. Maybe they prefer complicated explanations over the phone rather than email so they can ask probing questions, or maybe they prefer guidance at a high level over email but desire a face-to-face for follow up after they've had time to digest an email.

Everyone's unique in their approach to work. Your job as a successful corporate leader is to meet them where they are — not force them to assimilate to you — to set them up for success.

Personal Assessment

Self-discovery is an important element to being a successful corporate leader. I mentioned very early I don't know that many people who wake up one morning and announce to the world, "I'm going to be a leader someday." I know I didn't. An appetite for leadership is developed over time. Throughout the journey toward leadership, you'll discover your strengths and weaknesses naturally.

Books (like this one) will help you shortcut some potential mistakes. Maybe you aren't quite sure what your leadership tendencies are or how you best communicate. There are a variety of personality assessment tools that have proven useful for assessing strengths, personality traits, and work styles. The tools are meant to enhance self-awareness and will assist with self-discovery.

My advice is to explore a tool if it seems interesting to you, but don't take it for gospel. Use the information to help guide your interests and experiment. The tools can be a great assessment method for your employees if they aren't sure about their own leadership tendencies.

While there's some merit to the tools, proceed with caution. Your style will adapt and change over time. Check out different tools at different moments throughout your career, not only because your skills will improve, but also because societal expectations change as well.

I've heard anecdotal comments from seasoned employees whose results changed over time, and they were shocked at the differences. The bottom line is, there are several factors that will cause your style and methods to change, so make sure you maintain a growth mindset if you explore these assessments.

The three most popular assessments (and ones I've used) are:

- **DiSC**
- **CliftonStrengths**
- **Myers-Briggs**

Key Takeaways

1	Semantic, physical, physiological, and psychological noise can disrupt communication and lead to misunderstandings. Similarly, communication done through a low-context medium (e.g., text, email) can be less effective and more prone to misunderstanding than communication in a high-context medium (e.g., in person).
2	High-context communication depends on nonverbal communication and shared meaning. Nonverbal cues can consist of body language, eye contact, facial expression, gestures, noises, posture, proximity, and so on.
3	In all instances in which there's a potential for miscommunication due to the context or medium used, the best thing to do is slow down and ask for clarity when needed.
4	Be an active listener by being present and attentive; reflect on what someone's saying (rather than focusing on your response); clarify as needed, and when the conversation is ending, summarize the highlights of what you heard.
5	Never write down anything worse than something neutral. (And remember to assume best intent when reading something.)
6	Consider different communication mediums depending on the goal of what needs to be communicated. Share with your team how you prefer to communicate. Invite them to do the same so you can meet them where they are.
7	Consider personality assessment tools that assess strengths, personality traits, and work styles to learn more about how you and your team work, but remember that results could change over time.

Chapter 16:
Difficult Conversations

Different from both 1:1 meetings and performance improvement (PI) conversations, discussed in the last section, difficult conversations are in a class of their own. Difficult conversations arise when something needs to be addressed. They often occur when an employee said something or did something they shouldn't have, and you need to address it. Worst yet, a difficult conversation can occur because you're terminating an employee.

In the world of corporate leadership this often occurs when something has gone wrong, and discussions need to take place quickly. These are my least favorite types of conversations and require a leader to muster all their previous skill to conduct the conversation successfully. It's the class of conversation that really can make or break your success.

A difficult conversation will be a time to exercise **PARCS**, but I also have a few tips to **PAD** difficult conversations:

P RACTICE/PREPARE WHAT TO SAY

A VOID AVOIDANCE

D ON'T LISTEN TO RELOAD

Practice or Prepare What to Say

I don't think that leaders give enough credence to the value of practicing/preparing what to say in difficult conversations. When a "speech" must be given most people will practice, especially if the speech will be in front of a large audience. However, it's more detrimental to know exactly what you'll say in a difficult conversation than in a speech. Yet I've been part of difficult conversations in which it was clear that the message was not prepared in advance.

Especially important when discussing a policy violation or code of conduct violation, at minimum having a set of bullet points prepared is a must. You have no idea how the other person will react, and depending on their reaction, you could be completely thrown off your game plan.

Mike Tyson said it best, "Everyone has a plan until they get punched in the mouth." By no means am I indicating that you'll be susceptible to violence. However, a "punch" could come in the form of expletives directed at you, claims of racism, sexism or any other -ism, or a flat-out attack against your character. If the person you're speaking with is an aggressive communicator, I can guarantee you'll be on the receiving end of some expletives.

If you don't practice what you'll say or prepare bullets to keep on track, you could miss key points of your difficult conversation that could come back to haunt you, especially if those key points are legal requirements.

Avoid Avoidance

Having difficult conversations is my least favorite thing to do, but if you do the job for any significant amount of time, they will occur. As a leader, avoid avoidance. You just need to get on with it.

If you're facing a serious issue with an employee, avoiding the problem will only make it worse. If you allow a significant issue to carry on, you could be contributing to the creation of a toxic culture where one employee's shortcoming infects others. Avoid avoiding the conversation at all costs. Once you have cause for concern, practice and prepare what you'll say and get on with it. You and your organization will be better for it.

Don't Listen to Reload

Practice active listening — meaning don't listen only to reload your own response (see **Chapter 15: Communication Methods**). Not listening to reload is crucial during a difficult conversation.

You have no idea how a difficult conversation is going to go. If you start to get sucked into inflammatory comments directed your way, you'll start listening to reload with an attack. You can't let this happen in a difficult conversation. If you allow your emotions to go unchecked and make the conversation personal, you could lose all your standing.

Choose Your Moment

We all know that there's a time and a place for everything, and rarely does anything go according to plan. This is truer when serving as a successful corporate leader than it is for others. You may have concern, embrace authenticity, operate with realism, and express empathy, but if you don't choose the right moments to deliver difficult conversations, hold performance conversations, or even praise others, your efforts will be for naught.

This doesn't mean you need to tip-toe around, living in fear of saying the wrong thing at the wrong time. Like a teeter-totter, you'll constantly need to balance priorities with timing. Some actions require you to jump right in and address things immediately regardless of the surroundings. Others allow you to take your time to formulate the best strategy. An important part of expressing empathy is fostering a psychologically safe environment filled with trust. The best way to make that happen is to pick ideal times, locations, and the right communication medium appropriate for the message you need to deliver. You don't need to treat everyone with kid gloves, but you do need to have **CARE**.

	Key Takeaways
1	Practice or prepare what to say in a difficult conversation by at least making a list of the main points you need to communicate, but don't plan out every word you'll say — it's not a speech.
2	Avoid avoidance by getting on with difficult conversations when needed. Avoiding addressing a problem will only make it worse.
3	Practice active listening, and don't listen to reload.
4	Choose your moment to hold difficult conversations. Some issues may need to be addressed immediately, but some conversations can wait until a time and place that's a psychologically safe environment for the employee or you've been able to formulate a strategy to help address the problem.

Wrap Up
& Resources

Conclusion

What's been presented in *Lead with CARE* is a culmination of the knowledge attained from my own studies and the intentional experience gained from trial and error along the way. Behind the helpful acronyms exists the passion of a person who loves working with others and helping them reach their career goals. My hope is that you were able to gain a sense of that passion, and I've inspired your abilities as a successful corporate leader.

I can't say it enough, leadership is a **SURE** thing, and you need to make sure you're seriously ready to invest in your employees and show you **CARE**. I believe everything I presented in this book is attainable for those who have the right priorities and are truly interested in helping others.

For all the success I've attained, nothing was a solo effort and supporting valuable employees was key. I've said it before, I have a passion for leadership. I'm not always the best at it, but I always make my employees the priority.

I know there are other good leaders in the workplace. I also know there are bad leaders in the workplace. I sincerely believe that with the proper motivation, training via the principles of *Lead with CARE*, and hard work, you will be a successful corporate leader.

Becoming and remaining a successful corporate leader is a marathon, not a sprint. You'll have an opportunity to be a positive impact for those you interact with. Celebrate your wins along the way, especially when it means those wins are vicarious because your employees are crushing it.

Why Write This Book?

In 1997, two years out of high school, I was in California starting my first real job. I was a security guard at Adobe Systems HQ in downtown San Jose. Stepping into a corporate setting as a contractor was an amazing experience.

It was the first time I was given free drinks at work, had access to gourmet food, experienced a corporate holiday party, and was surrounded by amazing energy in my career. Somehow, I knew I'd end up working in corporate. Maybe they were unrealistic expectations at the time, but as the future would have it, I ended up working for three Fortune 500 companies.

After working two years with Adobe, I found myself in my first "official" career. In July 2000, I was sworn in as a police officer for the San Jose Police Department. As I started my career as a police officer, I knew it was the path I was destined to take. Not only did I meet my wife as I kicked off that career, but it was also the first job where I felt like I was part of a family.

I spent ten years with the police department. During that time, I dabbled in training arrest and control techniques, teaching firearms for a private organization, creating friend-ships, experiencing loss, and, most importantly, establishing the foundation for what would be my future in leadership.

It was the first environment where I recognized having concern for those I worked with was a powerful motivator. During the times I was placed in high-stress situations with lives on the line, be it the lives of fellow officers or citizens in need, it became apparent that my own needs melted away.

It didn't matter if I was tired, hungry, or afraid. When I was concerned for someone else, I could move mountains. I also learned what real empathy meant. Some of those harrowing calls for service meant I would arrive to a domestic violence situation, and a traumatized person just needed me to sit with them before speaking. Or it meant whisking away a frightened child who called because a parent was in medical distress, and they needed me to hold them as they bawled their eyes out on my shoulder.

No matter how long I was with the police department, responding to someone in need and consoling them after a traumatic event never got easier. However, it taught me that no matter the relationship, stranger or not, people respond when you express empathy by understanding their trauma and sharing your feelings.

In 2010, I left the police department and sought a new career. As destiny would have it, I found my way back into the corporate environment working as a security manager for a security contractor at the Apple campus in Cupertino, CA.

I'd been offered an amazing opportunity leading a small team doing shift work. I cherish the learning lessons and trial and error I experienced as I stumbled through the transition from working in the public sector to private. However, I learned early on that while I may not have had all the answers as a new corporate leader, if I kept CARE front of mind and treated my employees with respect, thus earning trust, I could achieve almost anything.

I quickly fell in love with leadership and knew I'd found my passion. I was eager to learn more and decided it was time to sharpen my leadership skills. It was time to seek the education I'd previously failed to attain.

I began pursuing a communications degree through Arizona State University. I was learning leadership and communication principles that allowed me to excel in my role, so much so that after one and a half years working as a contractor, I was officially hired as an Apple employee in 2012.

My destiny had come full circle from the Adobe days, and I was on top of the world. Little did I know that the following four years working with Apple would hone my leadership skills, allow me to experience even more success accompanied with some failure, and ultimately teach me the necessity for adhering to clearly defined leadership tenets.

During my time at Apple, I worked on several projects that stretched my expertise and exposed me to new and different aspects of not only corporate security as an industry but also the culture of a corporate tech company. Culture is an elusive target you must always be mindful of. I first realized the complexity of cultural consequences when I worked on developing operations in Shanghai, China. I learned valuable principles and practices the hard way.

The most memorable program I built was the foundation for Apple's Executive Protection (EP) Program. The development of the EP program was a challenge forever burned into my memory. I won't bore readers with the tedious details that made the work challenging and stressful all while affording me a once in a lifetime opportunity. However, I will highlight that for nearly two years of developing the program, I was exposed to an entirely new side of the corporate environment. I was thrust into working with and alongside the CEO of one of the largest companies in the world, and I had no idea what I was doing.

It was during this period that I honed my leadership style. When I was around Apple's CEO and his executive leadership team, I was a sponge. I wasn't paying attention to the confidential nature of conversations, instead I focused on how these leaders carried themselves.

I would note their style of communicating, openness during discussions, willingness to ask the hard questions, and, remarkably, their transparent vulnerability in not having all the answers. Most surprising of all was the amount of concern and empathy these senior leaders had for employees, consumers, and the environment.

The experience forever transformed my approach to leadership in a corporate environment and strengthen my resolve that CARE was a foundation successful corporate leaders should have.

As life dictates, all things must come to an end. In summer 2016, for the first time I knew what burnout was. In my six years at Apple, I'd completed my bachelor's degree, traveled all over the world, developed multiple programs for Apple that still exist to this day, and managed hundreds of employees and contractors. All those accomplishments, yet I was experiencing imposter syndrome, my marriage was suffering, and I'd lost my love for the work.

I took a three-month sabbatical to realign my priorities in life. Aside from marrying my wife, it was one of the best decisions I've made in my life. Realizing the power of stepping away, I discovered the value of exercising mindfulness on a regular basis.

During those three months of stepping away from the workplace, I spent quality time with my wife and sons, studied for the GMAT (which I never ended up taking), took a police officer re-qualification course, and realigned my priorities. I rekindled the spark and passion that I had for leading teams and found another company to partner with. Destiny pulled me back into the corporate environment at Meta (then Facebook).

In fall 2016, I started with Meta. I found myself working on several large projects and managing another large team of employees. However, one major difference was my exposure to a leader who would forever change my perspective on corporate leadership.

For the first time in a corporate environment, I felt invested in as an employee. At first, the experience felt abnormal. There I was in a corporate security organization expecting leadership to be as I'd previously experienced, and I was taken aback that my leader was investing in my growth and development. It was a whole new world and one that I didn't realize I was craving.

In two years working for Meta, I was reminded of the value of open communication but also learned the need to challenge status quo, investing in performance development (through performance management and performance enablement), and knowing when to act on the behalf of others (allyship).

The opportunities I was afforded at Meta were among the most beneficial to my leadership development, but destiny once again reared its head, and I was offered an opportunity that I couldn't pass up.

In fall 2018, I started a management position with Google. The opportunity at Google allowed me to work on global programs all over the world. The following five years, COVID-19 notwithstanding, were an amazing opportunity and rounded out my experience and expertise by providing me with true global management experience. In January 2023, I was affected by the tech layoffs, bringing my time at Google to an end.

While still at Google in December 2020, I completed my Master of Science in Applied Leadership and Management with Thunderbird School of Global Management from Arizona State University (ASU).

A blessing in disguise, leaving Google gave me an opportunity to fully invest in completing my doctoral dissertation. In December 2023, I completed my doctorate, becoming a Doctor of Education in Organizational Change and Leadership with the University of Southern California (USC).

The culmination of my passion, failures, experience, and education led to putting my thoughts into words creating *Lead with CARE*.

Acronym Glossary

ACE — p. 63

The best way to promote others and provide opportunity is being a champion for DEI initiatives and an ACE at breaking down barriers:

- **Acknowledge inequity**
- **Change interactions**
- **Embrace diversity**

ADD — p. 53

I have three simple rules to ADD authenticity when it comes to exercising DEI in the workplace:

- **Accept everyone**
- **Don't fake it**
- **Do be present**

ALPINE — p. 98

You can reach the lofty ALPINE heights by:

- **Acting**
- **Learning**
- **Pivoting**
- **Implementing**
- **Never giving up**
- **Evaluating**

BEAM — p. 116

Improve your leadership skills to be real with your employees and BEAM DOOD:

- **Be present**
- **Exercise mindfulness**
- **Acknowledge career stagnation**
- **Manage by walking around (MBWA)**
- **Door open, open door (DOOD) policy**

BLINC — p. 112

When developing your own VMO, these five considerations will help you create goals in a BLINC of an eye that are:
- **Broad**
- **Linked**
- **Inclusive**
- **Nimble**
- **Considerate**

CARE — p. 4

The primary philosophy of my book is that all successful corporate leaders should have CARE as their raison d'être (reason for being):
- **Concern**
- **Authenticity**
- **Realism**
- **Empathy**

CRAFT — p. 162

I have some tips that can help CRAFT a positive environment, enabling those with either a growth or fixed mindset to succeed:
- **Create an environment where failure is allowed and accepted**
- **Respond in times of adversity**
- **Acknowledge difficulty**
- **Focus on strengths**
- **Track progress**

DREAM — p. 36

You can act ethically with five simple principles and be the DREAM of ethical leadership with:
- **Direct communication**
- **Role modeling**
- **Equitable decision-making**
- **Allyship**
- **Managing with integrity**

ESCAPE — p. 150

Remember that sometimes we all need understand how to ESCAPE a full cognitive load:

- **Emergencies happen**
- **Self-awareness**
- **COVID-19 is endemic**
- **Away means away**
- **Practice what you preach**
- **Employee assistance programs (EAP)**

FUN — p. 144

I hope that you'll find the FUN in your performance improvement (PI) conversations with these three tips:

- **Future focused**
- **Understand career goals**
- **Not a normal 1:1**

JEMS — p. 118

Mindfulness can be as valuable as JEMS, by:

- **Journaling**
- **Exercising**
- **Meditating**
- **Stepping away**

PAD — p. 191

I have a few tips to PAD difficult conversations:

- **Practice/prepare what to say**
- **Avoid avoidance**
- **Don't listen to reload**

PARCS — p. 182

By implementing five easy steps, active listening will be like taking a walk through the PARCS:

- **Present**
- **Attentive**
- **Reflect**
- **Clarify**
- **Summarize**

PUGS — p. 158

Performance enablement can be as dependable as PUGS:

- **Performance review**
- **Understanding human capital**
- **Growth vs. fixed mindset**
- **SMART goals**

SMART — p. 165

The easiest and most efficient way to create a goal is ensuring it's SMART:

- **Specific**
- **Measurable**
- **Achievable**
- **Relevant**
- **Time-bound**

SURE — p. 11

People management is a SURE thing. It's:

- **Selfless**
- **Unending**
- **Rewarding**
- **Exhausting**

TACK — p. 51

Like a boat navigating through wind, you will forge ahead with DEI, knowing TACK:

- **Traditional approaches don't work**
- **Allyship**
- **Creating opportunities**
- **Knowing your limits**

TAPE — p. 16

Vulnerability should hold your organization together like TAPE through:

- **Trust**
- **Asking for help**
- **Prioritizing your needs**
- **Entrusting your team to deliver**

TRUST — p. 138

Productive 1:1 meetings are a time to focus on TRUST:

- **Timely**
- **Resolve roadblocks**
- **Updates**
- **Set expectations and seek clarification**
- **Truthful**

Resources

Bibliography

Doran, George T. "There's a S.M.A.R.T. way to write management's goals and objectives." *Management Review*, Nov. 1981, pp. 35-36.

Hofstede, Geert. *Culture's Consequences: Comparing Values, Behaviors, Institutions and Organizations Across Nations.* Sage Publications, 2001.

Holden, Ginny. "15 Vince Lombardi quotes to inspire IT pros." *The Enterprisers Project*, Red Hat, Inc., 26 Jan. 2015, enterprisersproject.com/article/2015/1/
15-vince-lombardi-quotes-inspire-cios-and-it-pros.

"The GLOBE Studies." *GLOBE (Global Leadership and Organizational Behavior Effectiveness).* https://globeproject.com/studies.

About the Author

Dr. Ely Albalos is an expert in leadership and business management with over 20 years of progressive leadership in global program management, large-scale corporate security management, law enforcement, entrepreneurship, and organizational change for three Fortune 500 companies.

Ely has led the security teams of some of the largest corporations in the world, including Apple, Facebook, and Google. As well as functioning as a CEO for a startup in the money services business, he hosts a regular motivational podcast and blog named *Ely's Echo*. Ely is passionate about helping others, and he hopes to help people navigate the complexity of leadership and business management.

As a lifelong learner, Ely has a Master's in Applied Leadership & Management and received a doctorate in Organizational Change & Leadership at the University of Southern California in 2023.

Lion Consulere — We Care

Leveraging over 60 years of combined experience in the workforce, Lion Consulere founders are inspired to share their learning lessons. Having worked in a gambit of environments from the public sector in law enforcement to the private sector in Fortune 100 companies, the founders use their collective expertise to help others shortcut the path toward success. Lion Consulere cares about making information accessible and digestible for everyone. In this fourth industrial revolution there is no reason skills for personal, career, and business success can't be shared with the masses. It only takes the smallest spark of desire to ignite the flame for determination. Lion Consulere is ready to receive those who are determined to learn, grow, and develop. Let our passion for caring carry over into your life.

Ely's Echo

In this blog and podcast you'll discover my attempt at sharing original thoughts, insight/opinions on leadership, current events in society, an inside look into my unique experiences, and random posts that just allow me to inspire via the written word. Ultimately, I do hope that readers are able to connect with my blog, and I hope to be inspired by all of you as well. I will always do my best to write well but not be so precise that I sacrifice substance for structure.

Acknowledgements

I was just beginning my second year with the University of Southern California (USC), walking out of my home office after finishing an evening class. As was becoming the norm for class nights, my wife was just finishing preparing dinner in the kitchen, so we could dine together. As I entered the kitchen, she looked at me and asked, "What's wrong?"

Some of the USC academic content had become strenuous and even emotionally draining when studying ethnic and racial inequity, so my wife's question had become ritualistic most class nights. However, on that night, I had something else on my mind. I simply responded, "I really wish the organizations I worked for had access to the information I'm learning."

With the insightful conversations and useful educational material I was absorbing, I felt as if I were being exposed to a whole new level of leadership. If the organizations I worked for had implemented even a fraction of the leadership methods and models for employees like me, then people could've had a whole new relationship with their work. While we ate dinner, I rambled on for thirty minutes about different ways employees could be engaged and empowered in the workplace, citing research, and even using examples from my work experience to create realistic applications.

My wife, patient as ever, listened to every word and at the end uttered one sentence that addressed the elephant in the room, "You know what you have to do right?" Then and there, the creation of *Lead with CARE* was set into motion.

It's not with humility, but instead with pure honesty that I acknowledge *Lead with CARE* would never have been written had it not been for my wife's contribution and never-ending support. I also thank her for helping me identify and recognize the true reason I enjoy leadership — my Tata (my grandfather).

As I developed *Lead with CARE*, many times I found myself reflecting on the source of my passion for helping others. My Tata was the father figure in my life. As the head of our family, he put everyone's needs before his own. Often the first to wake up and start work for the day and the last to be seated at the table for a meal, my Tata's actions taught me what sacrifice for others meant. My only regret is I can't thank him for his contributions to my life in helping me become the leader I am today. I hope that as he looks down on me from heaven, he can smile knowing his life lessons are with me, and his legacy is passed along in *Lead with CARE*.

Praise for *Lead with CARE*

"True leadership is only valuable if you can help others to be their best while accomplishing shared organizational goals. *Lead with CARE* is a practical and tactical guide on how to approach this leadership challenge. *Lead with CARE* provides new leaders concrete steps to get started building a solid foundation and explains WHY these moves are so important to a leader's overall impact."

– Dr. Stefanie Phillips, CEO, Chamberlin Education Foundation

"Ely shares his real-world leadership examples and challenges while also providing solutions for successful outcomes. Improve your leadership skills with simple but powerful tools used by successful leaders. *Lead with CARE* is a handbook for those at any level of their professional journey. Non-managers, managers, and tenured leaders will find useful tools to adapt to their own leadership style are and improve their engagement with others. I highly recommend this book to anyone interested in leadership as a topic of learning or greater understanding."

– John R. Day, Corporate Security Professional, Law Enforcement Chief (Retired)

"A fantastic read to *Lead with CARE* from a proven results-driven professional who has paved the path to success at multiple major Silicon Valley companies. I take great pride in having worked alongside Ely at one of them. I highly recommend this valuable book to newbies and seasoned professionals who seek to initiate or polish a corporate team mentality via Ely's CARE ideology, which can certainly drive success in both simple and industry-shaping projects."

– Christopher Salgado, CEO, All Points Investigations, LLC

"*Lead with CARE* nails the essential principles and traits for successful corporate leadership. The importance of thoughtful meetings and building trust are broken down to help readers understand the benefits of open communication, while recognizing one's cognitive limits. By fostering these approaches, leaders can affect excellence in others."

> – Steve Krystek, CEO, PFC Safeguards, PFC Group of Companies

"Ely's journey to becoming the people leader he is today has fostered the development of a distinct and effective leadership style. His experiences, both tried and tested, offer invaluable insights for us to refine and enhance our own leadership techniques. Furthermore, his thoughtfully crafted acronyms and insightful chapter summaries provide practical tools that can be immediately applied, assisting in the cultivation of our own unique leadership styles. I highly recommend *Lead with CARE* to any aspiring or existing people leader who seeks to lead with authenticity and care."

> – Carlos Galvez, Vice President of Global Security and Financial Intelligence Unit